Burmese Gaze

Portraits from Burma 1988/2009

Photography by Philip J. Bigg

Burmese Gaze
Portraits from Burma 1988/2009

Photography by Philip J. Bigg

The photographs in this book first appeared in May 2011 at
Velvet Goldmine Studio, Brighton as part of the Brighton Festival
curated by Aung San Suu Kyi.

www.velvetgoldminestudio.com
www.philipjbigg.com
www.burmacampaign.org.uk

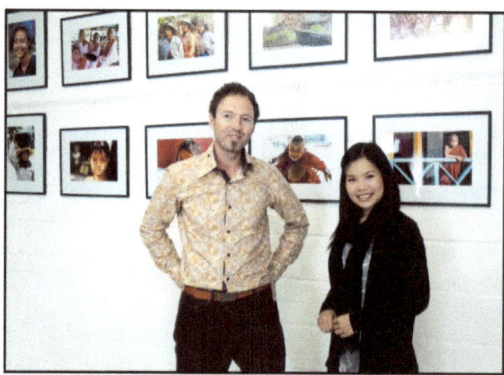

Philip J. Bigg is pictured with Zoya Phan, a high profile
Burmese refugee and pro-democracy campaigner for
Burma Campaign UK who visited the exhibition at
Velvet Goldmine Studio in May 2011.

PANSODAN BOOKS

I'm a "people" photographer, but I prefer recording people unawares, capturing the unprepared moment, the unposed, unsmiling, natural shots.
Most of the time I use a 200mm zoom, but sometimes even that is not far enough away to remain unnoticed.

Taking someone's photograph is an invasion of their personal space.
I have a "shoot first, plead ignorance afterwards" approach.
Asking first will kill the moment and destroy what may have been a great photograph.

The eyes are said to be the gateway to the soul; you'll always tell a person's well-being through their eyes.
Another belief is that taking a person's image means that you are stealing or taking away part of their soul.

As a photographer I am always having a personal battle with myself on whether I am doing wrong.
I wonder if I am being too intrusive.
On my first trip to India in 1987, a Tibetan man ran after me asking if I had taken his photograph.
He looked so threatening that I said that I hadn't.
Pre-digital he could not check, but that stood me in good stead for always being wary whenever I raised my camera to my eye.

You can normally tell if someone does not want their photograph taken.
They will look or turn away, gesture or swear at you. Or even throw objects.
That is a certain "No".
I always respect that and walk away.
Some days it doesn't always work out.
Maybe I am lacking self-confidence or in the wrong mood.
There is no point shooting on those days.

I first went to Burma/Myanmar in 1988. I was travelling around South East Asia and having read encouraging travel articles, decided to visit Burma.
My knowledge of the country was lacking. I knew nothing political.
My memories of visiting Burma then were feelings of suppression.

At the time I visited, there were a series of marches and protests that became known as the "Four-Eights Uprising," as it was initiated on 8-8-88.

I had no idea what the people were going through, as there were nightly curfews and few discussed what was happening with foreigners.

Thousands of monks, students and other civilians demonstrating against the government of the time were killed, and the uprising led to the country being ruled again by the military. But to the outsider the people seemed happy enough so you would not have guessed that there were problems.

The new military rulers agreed to hold multi-party elections.

Although Aung San Suu Kyi's party, the National League for Democracy (NLD) won the election in 1990, the results were not recognised by the junta and she remained under house arrest for years, released from time to time, only to be detained again until a more convincing release in November 2010.

Since then the party has been legally dissolved, then legally registered, and won all but one seat in it's first contest, a by-election.

In 2009 I visited for the second time.

It was still a marathon task getting up at four in the morning to catch buses and trucks, sharing the rear with multiple packs of plant fertiliser, staying in comfortless guest houses, offering similar bland variations of what they could do with an egg.

I was exhausted and starved of home comforts, decent food and subject as all are, to frequent power cuts.

But it was all worth it for four weeks, especially considering the issues the Burmese people have been subjected to and endure daily.

I was trying my best to support the local people.

And what a joy the people are.

Everywhere I went there was hearty welcomes and big smiles.

Forget Thailand, marketed as "the land of smiles," whose people are positively moody in comparison with the Burmese.

I do not know another country where visitors receive the same welcome.

So has the country changed over 21 years?

People were more willing to converse with me in public this time around.

Whereas in 1988 I was granted a 7-day visa and could only visit the three main areas of Rangoon, Mandalay and Pagan, by 2009 a monthly visa was standard issue,

allowing me to explore more, although there are still restricted areas in the conflicted zones.

Generally the country has developed pretty slowly in comparison with the countries it borders.

You won't find Starbucks or McDonalds, the infrastructure is basic, the roads are somewhat potholed and the internet and cable TV connections are pretty erratic.

But the people are the real draw.

For this book I have selected images where I have obtained the person's permission first.

Mostly.

Nations have different attitudes to being photographed.

Some are more photo friendly than others.

I felt particularly self conscious in Burma.

It is a sensitive country with internal conflict that affected my psyche.

The Burmese people are still approachable despite their hardship and I managed to capture some great portraits.

For the majority, I have engaged with my subject and made a connection with them.

I regard these as some of my finest portraits.

If you can live with a few hardships and desire seeing a country that is unique and has retained a village-like charm for the past twenty years,

then do not think twice about visiting this enchanting place.

One day I shall return to the country, seek out the people that I photographed in the past and reconnect with them.

Philip J. Bigg
May 2011

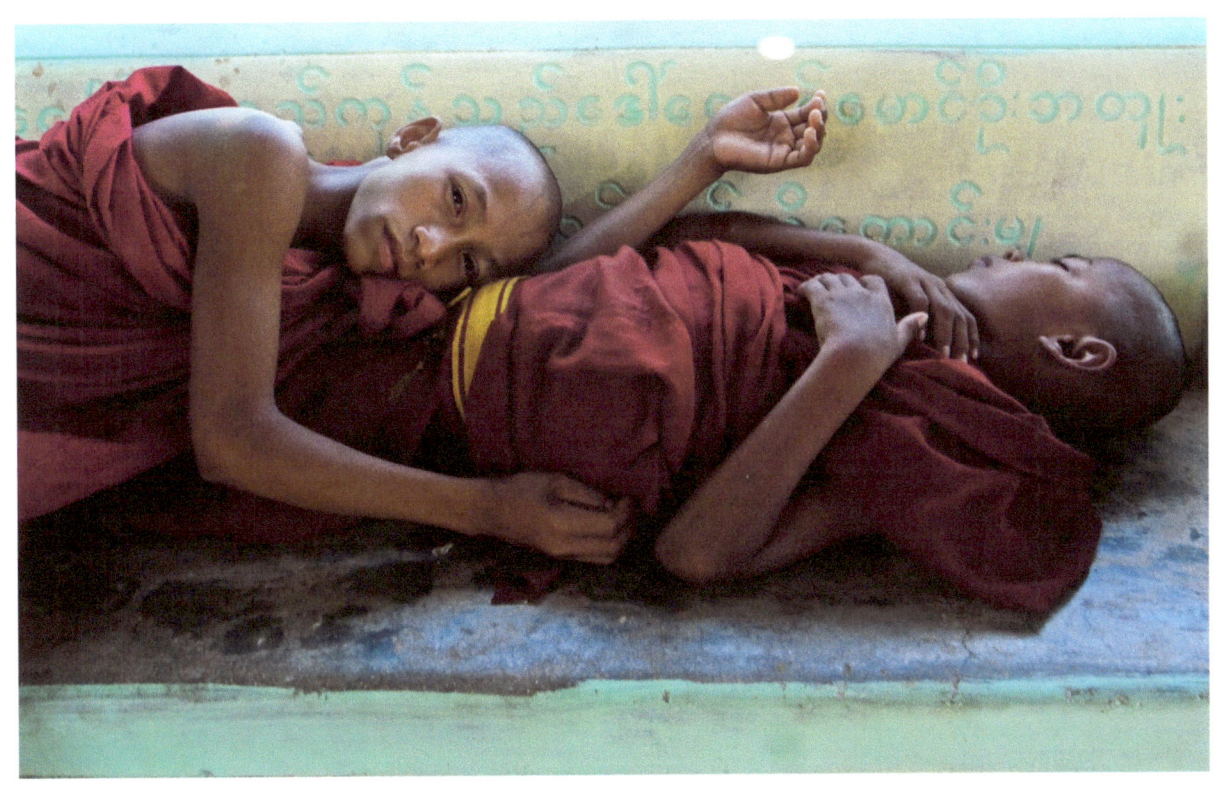

Novice monks sleeping, Sagaing Temple, Mandalay, 2009

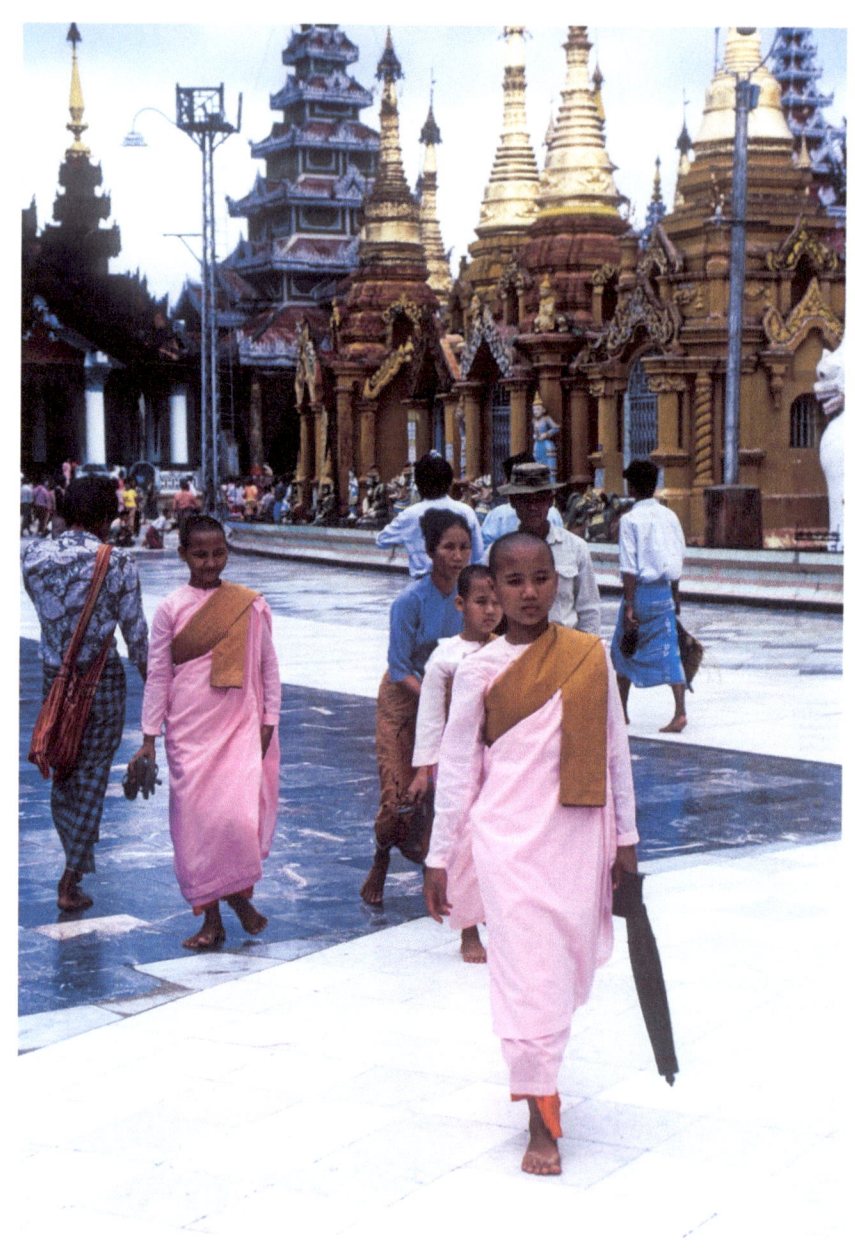

Young Nuns at Shwedagon Pagoda, Yangon, 1988

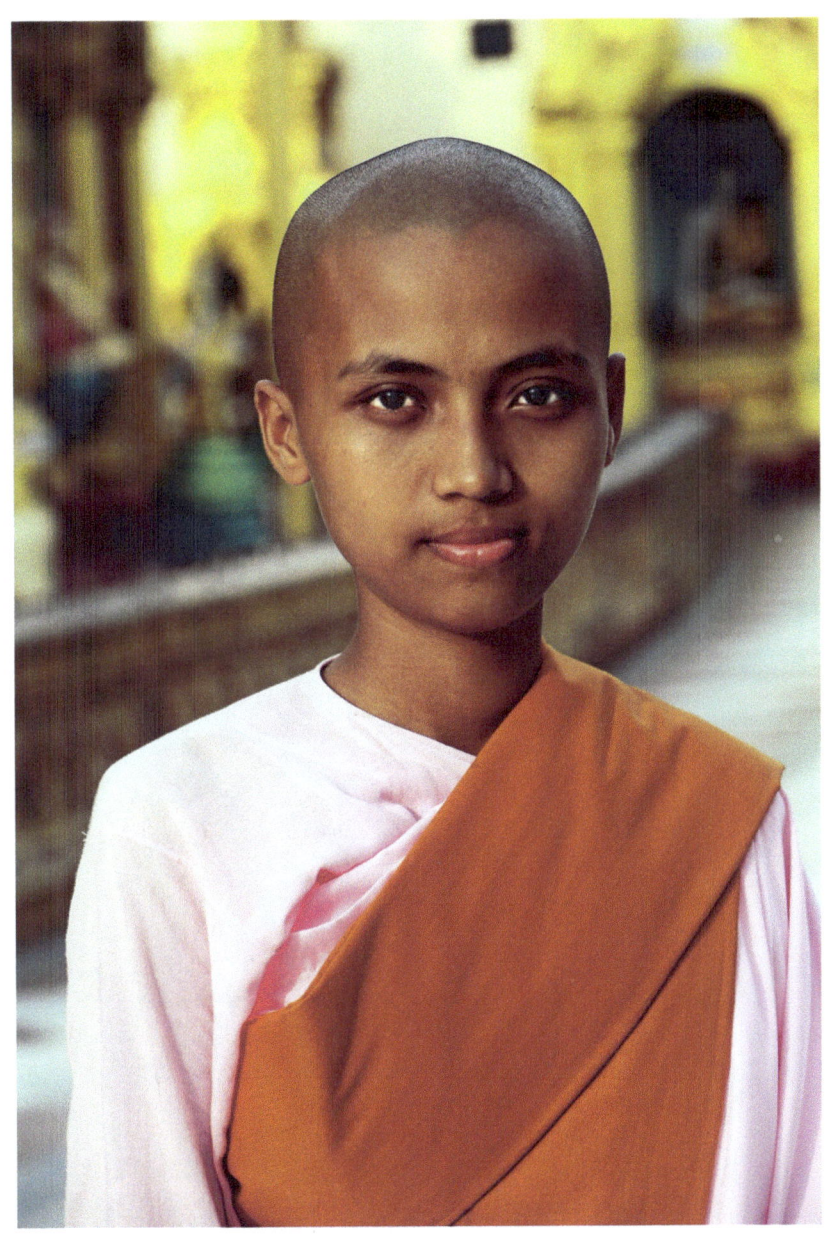

Young Nun at Shwedagon Pagoda, Yangon, 2009

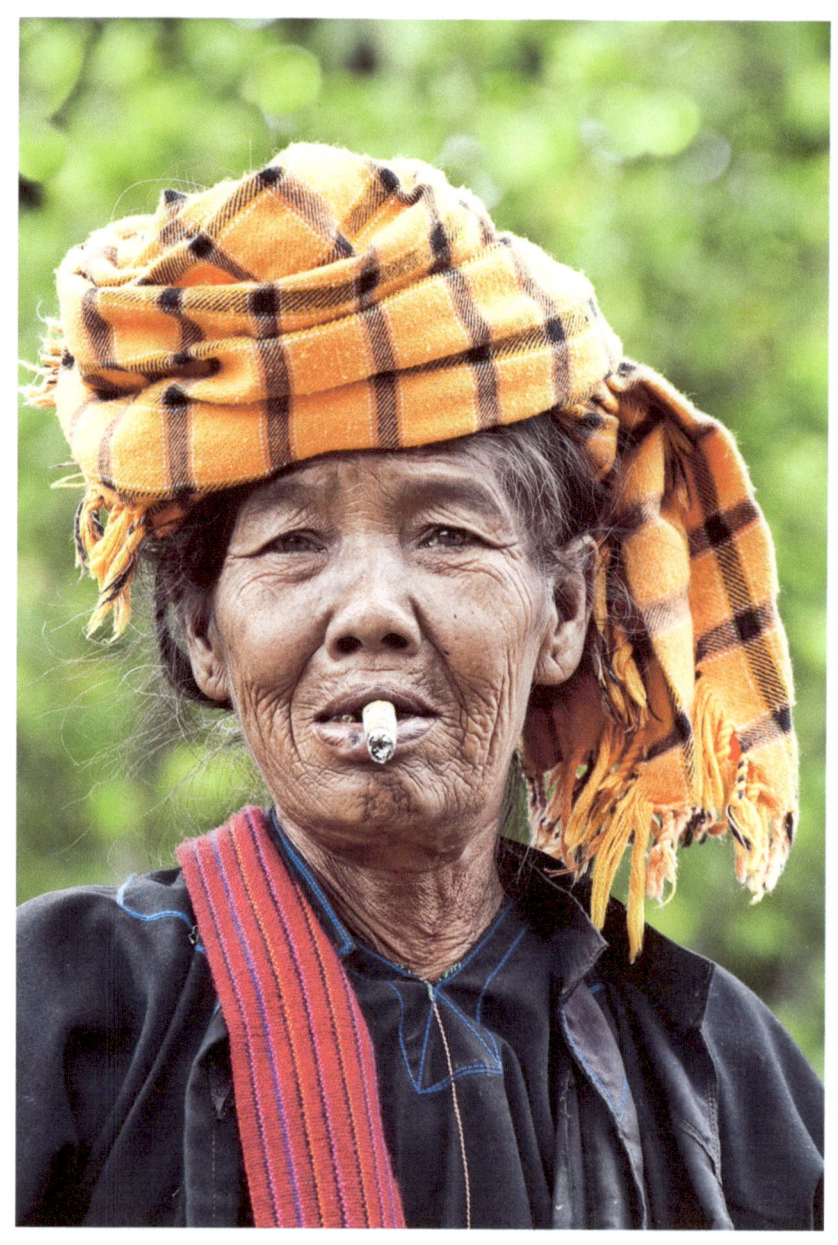

Cigar Smoking Market Trader, Kalaw, Inle Lake, 2009

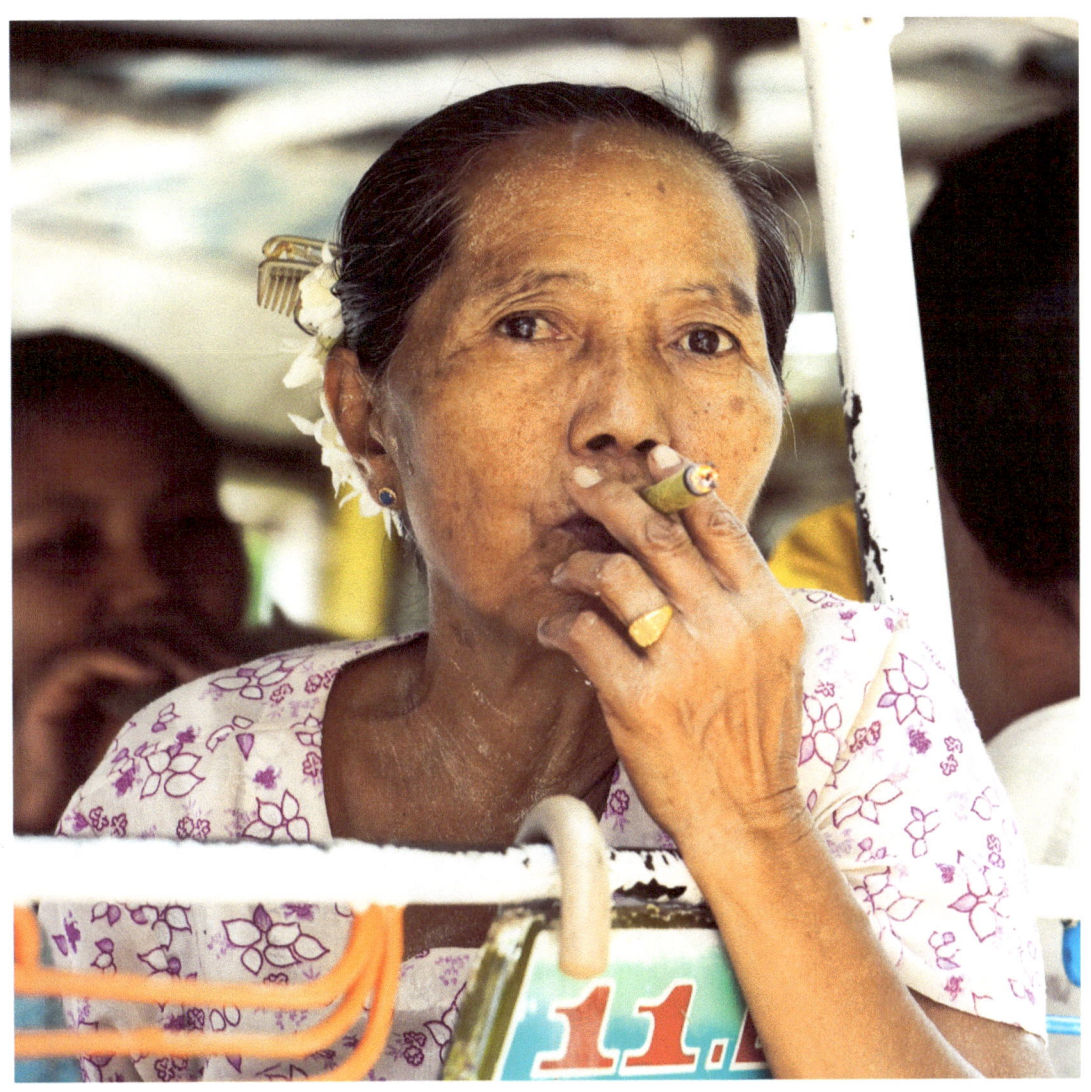

Cigar Smoker on local bus, Monywa, 2009

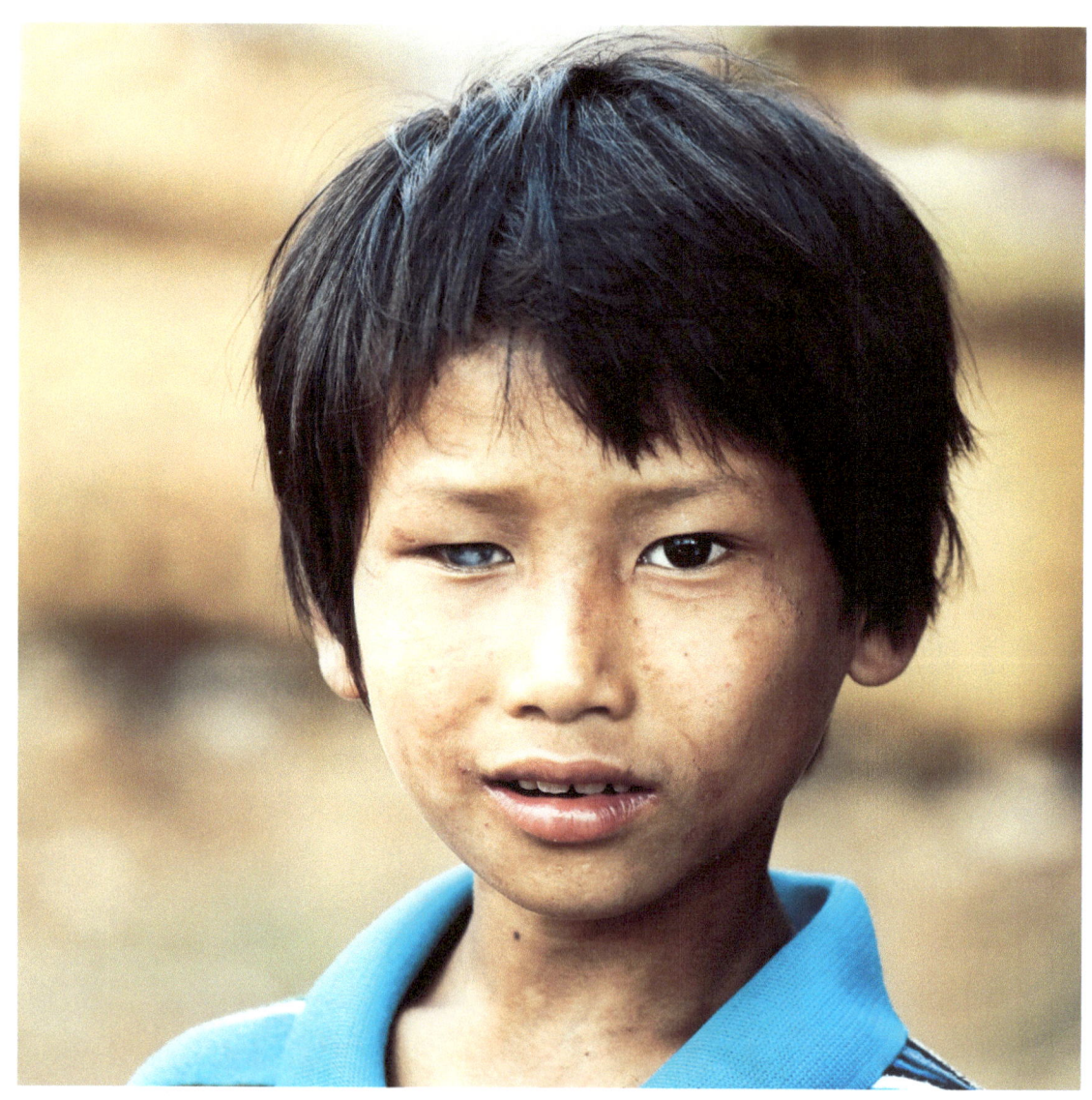

Boy with cataract, Maing Thauk, Inle Lake, 2009

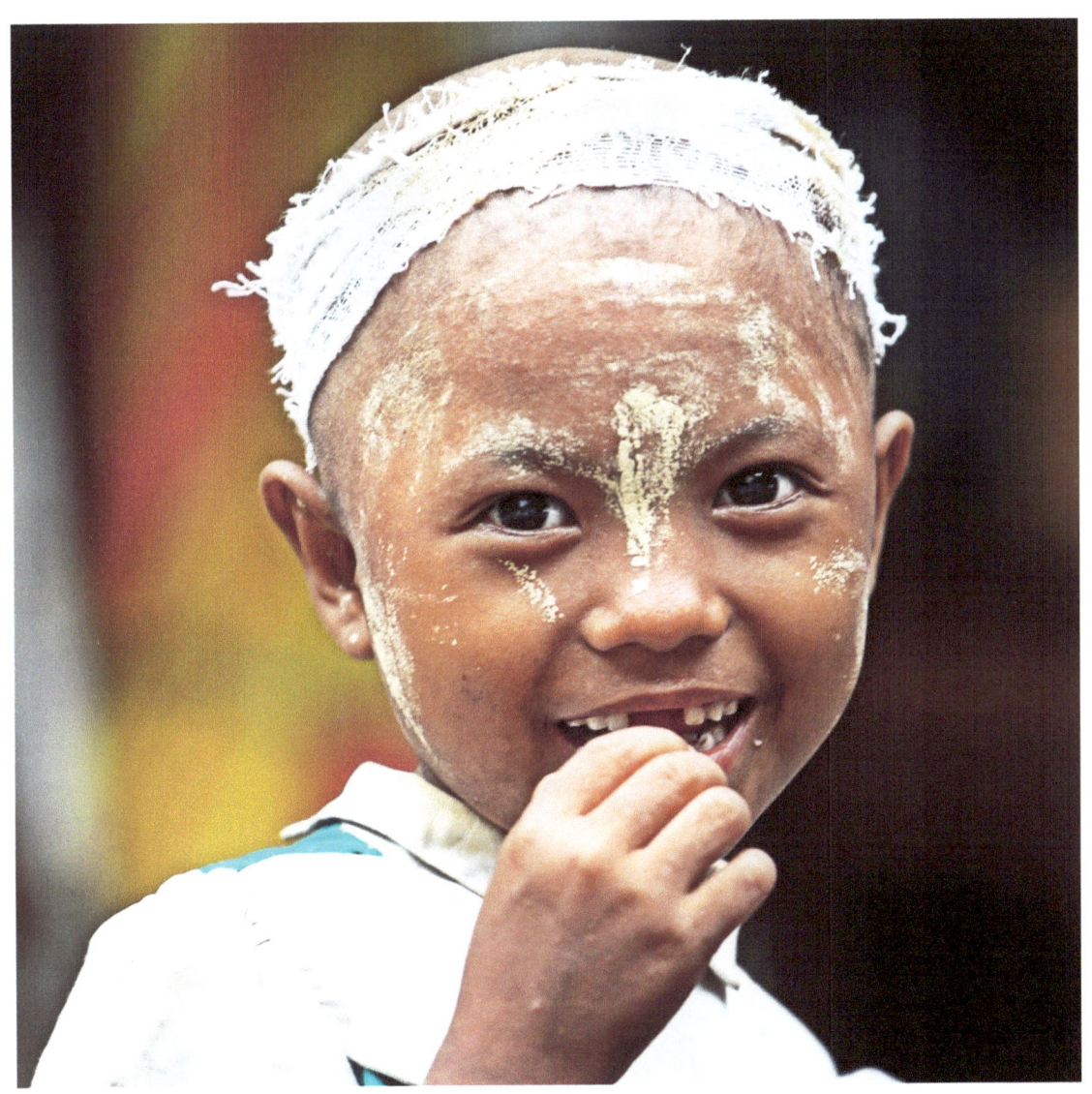

Child in street with head wound, Yangon, 2009

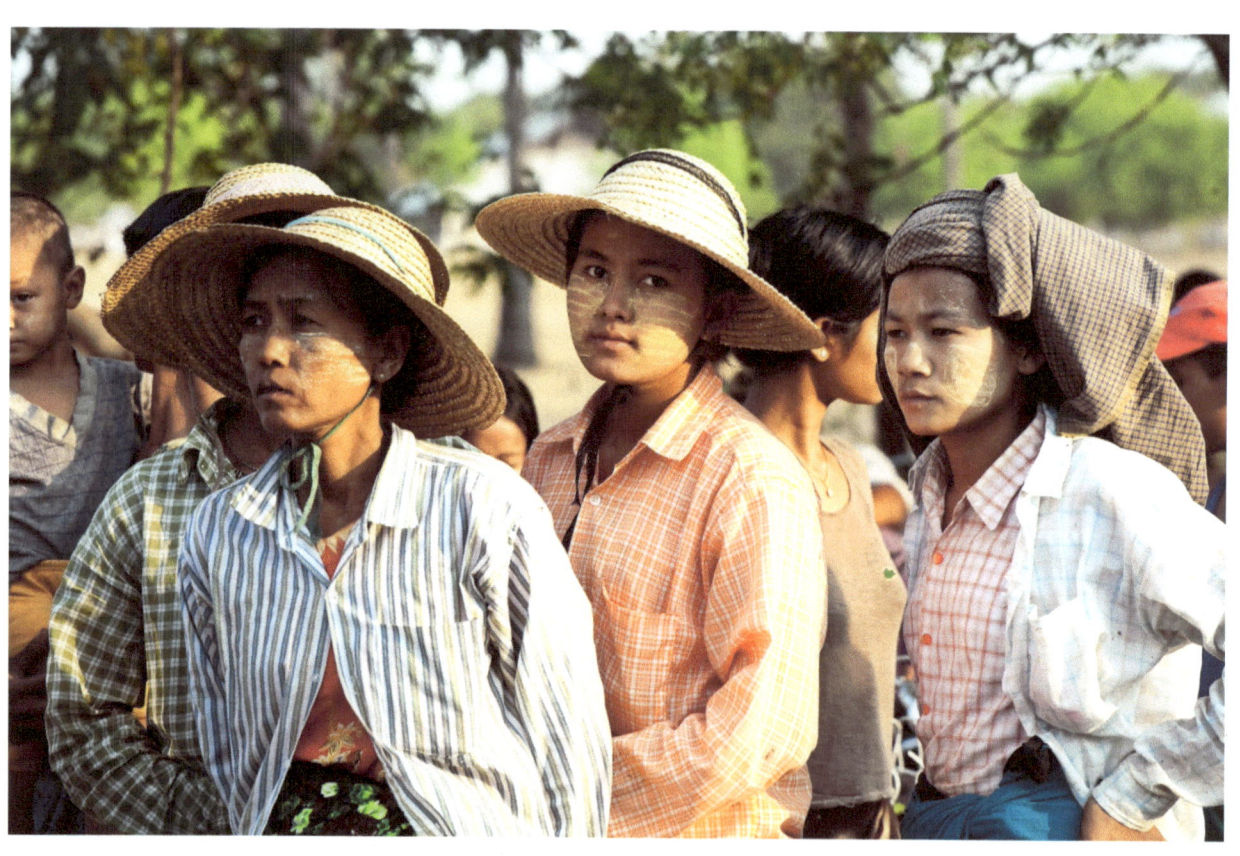

Labourers watching funeral procession, Bagan, 2009

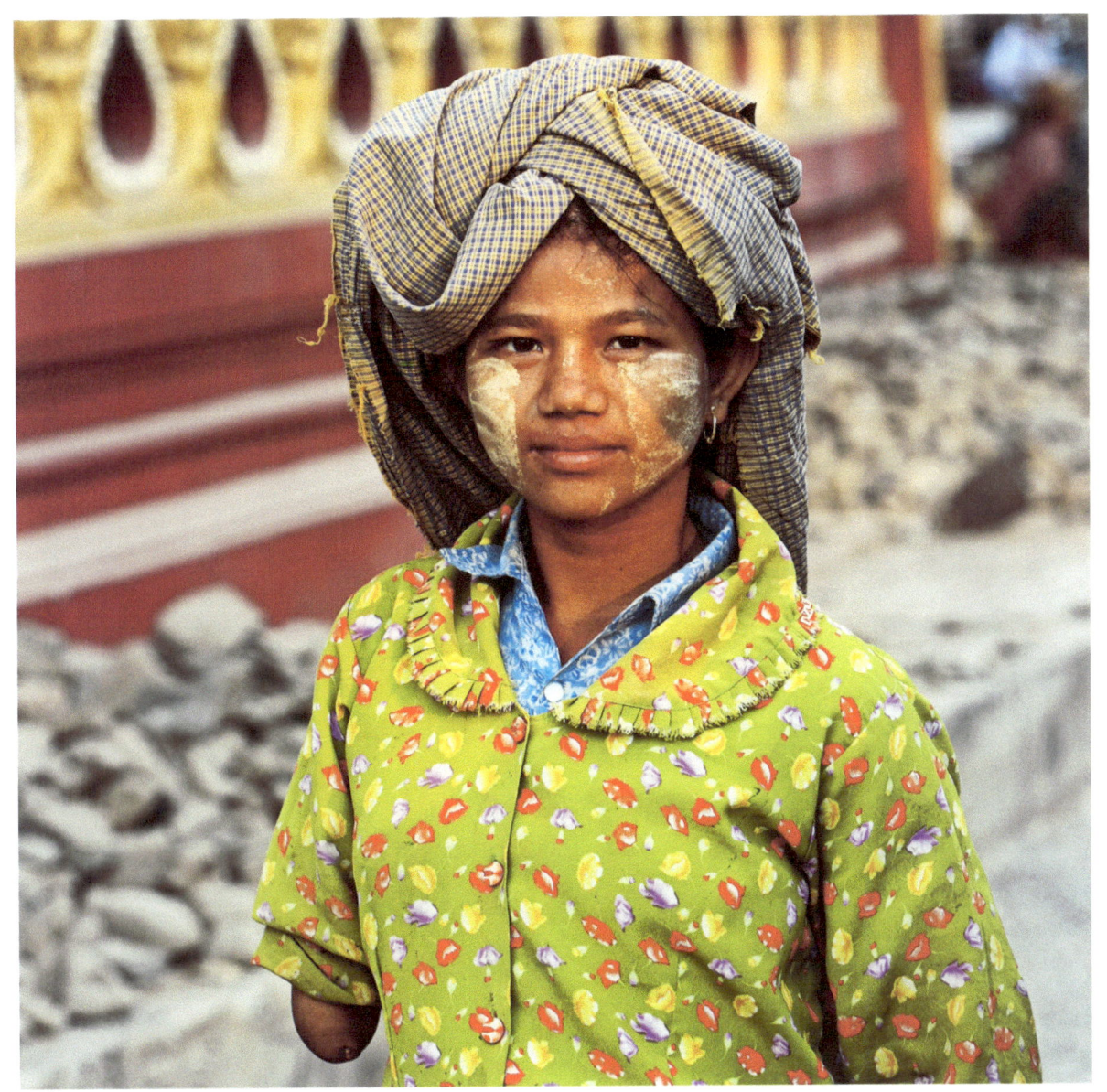

One armed labourer working on roads, Monywa, 2009

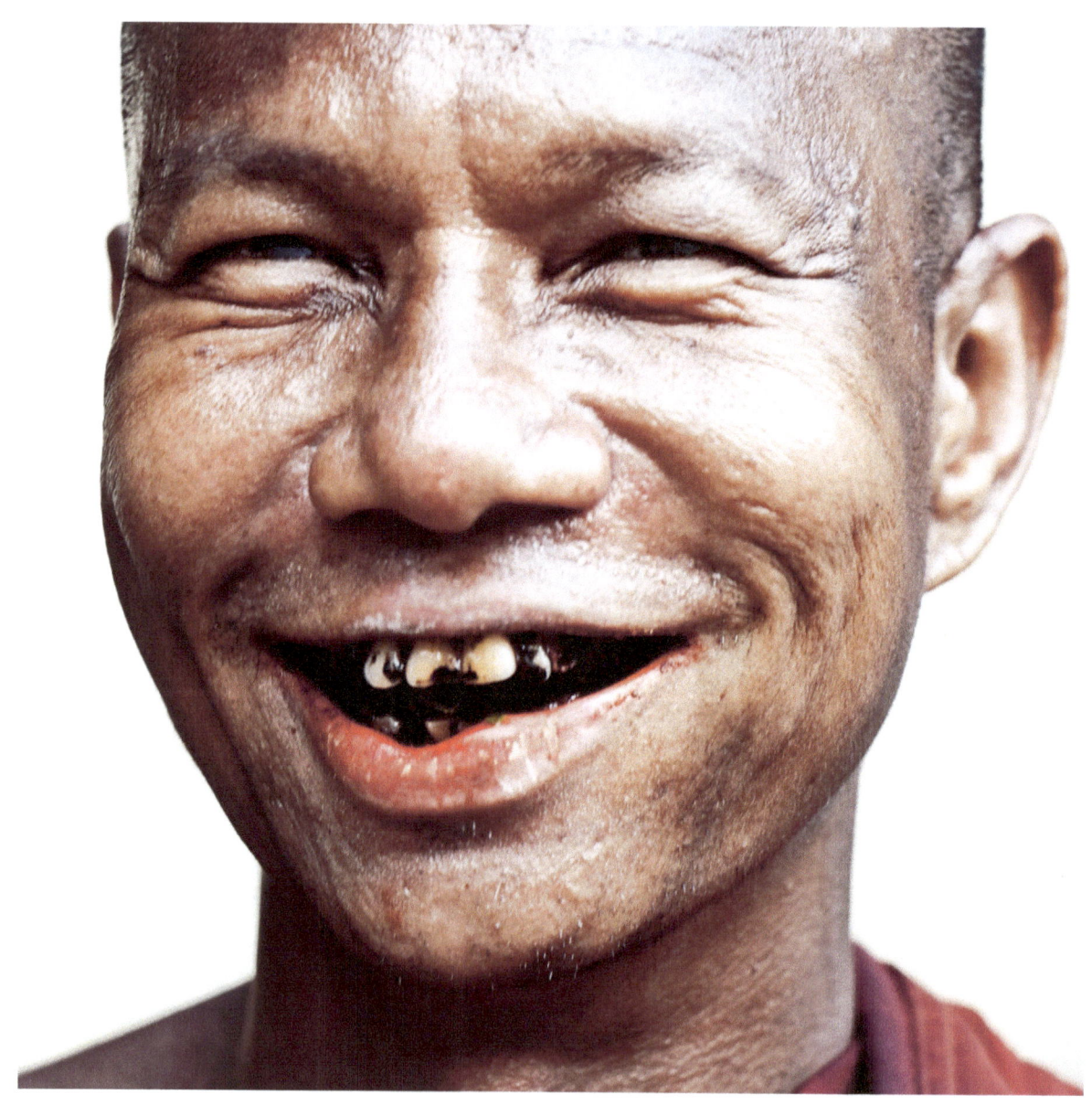

Betel nut chewing monk, Mandalay, 2009

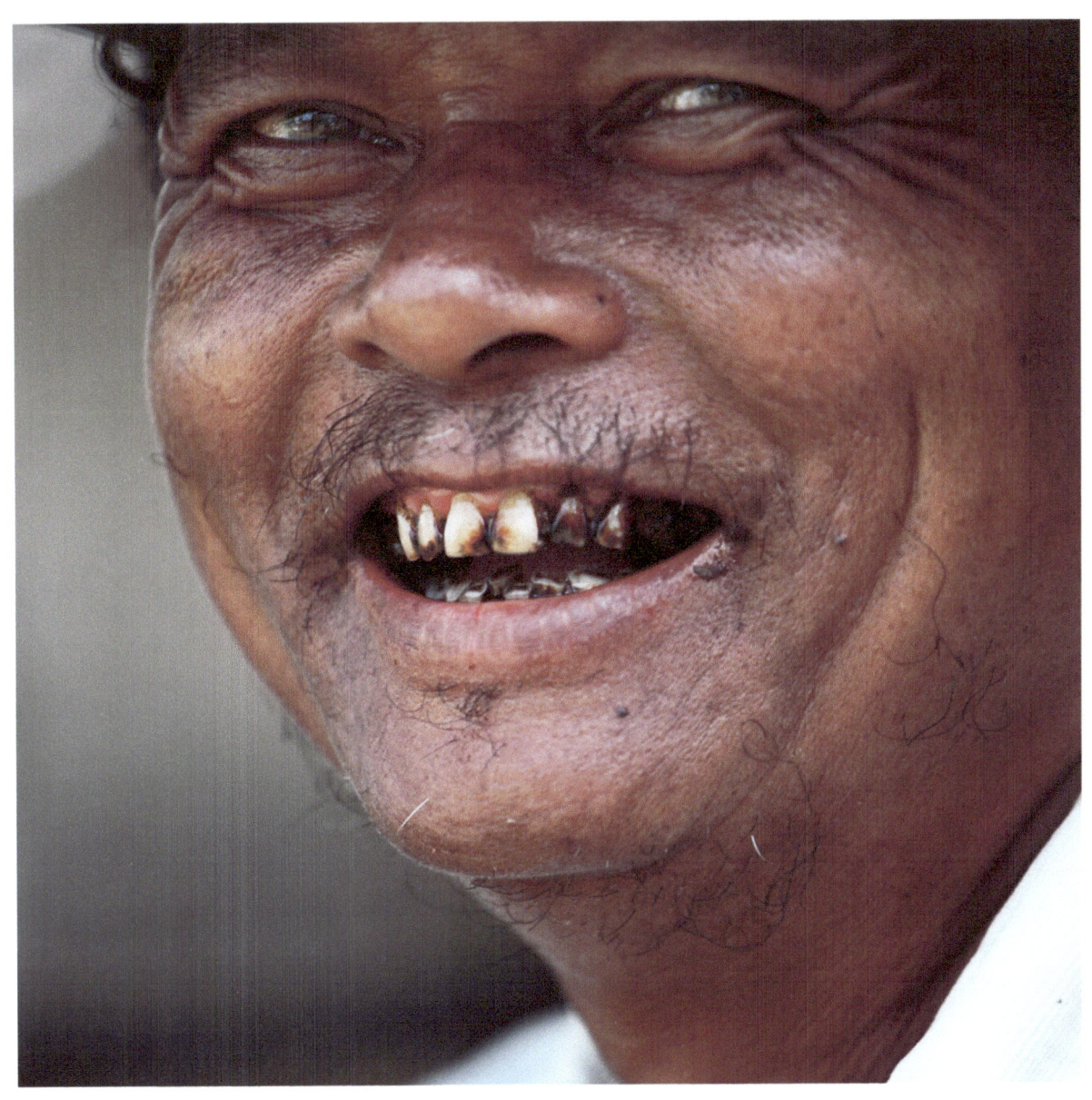

Betel nut chewing market trader, Maing Thauk, Inle Lake, 2009

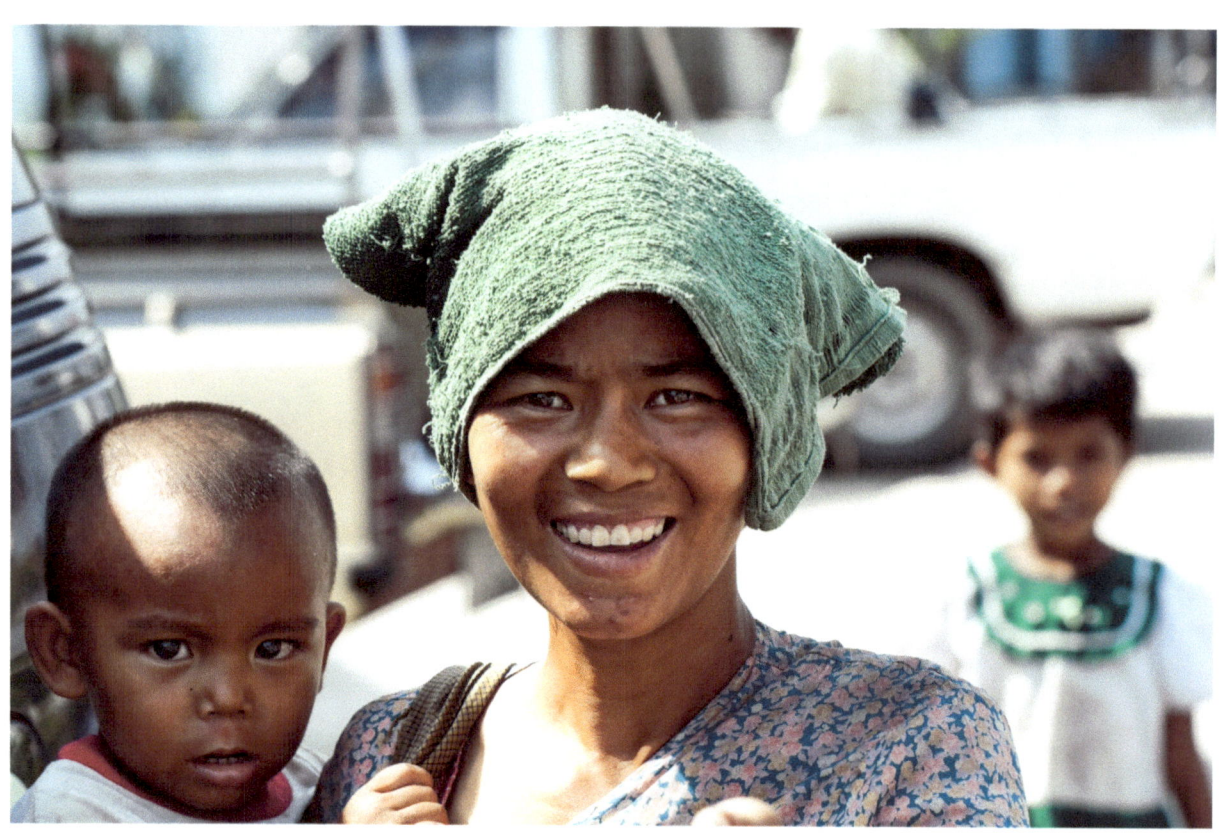

Mothers with children begging outside restaurant, Mandalay, 2009

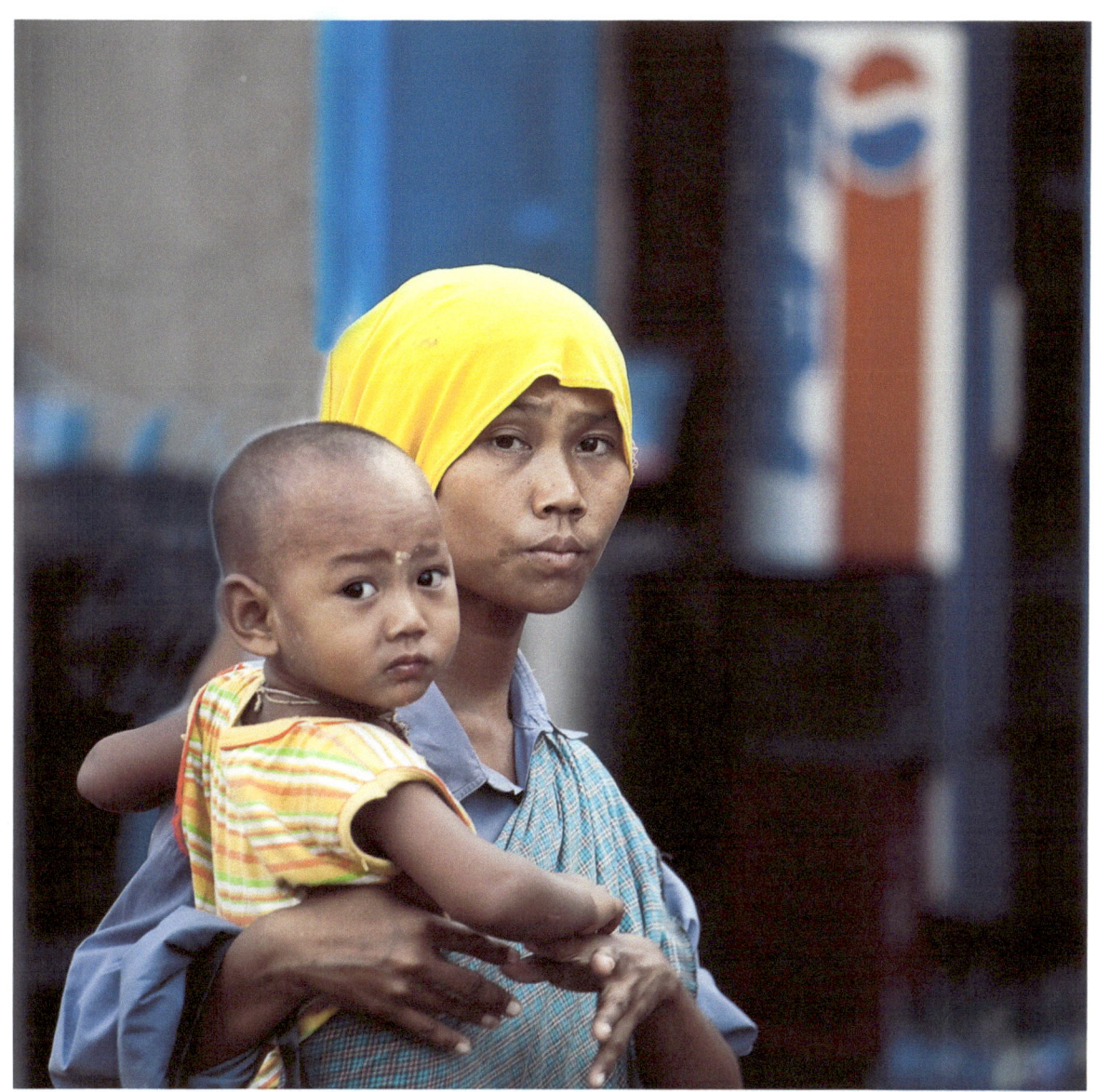

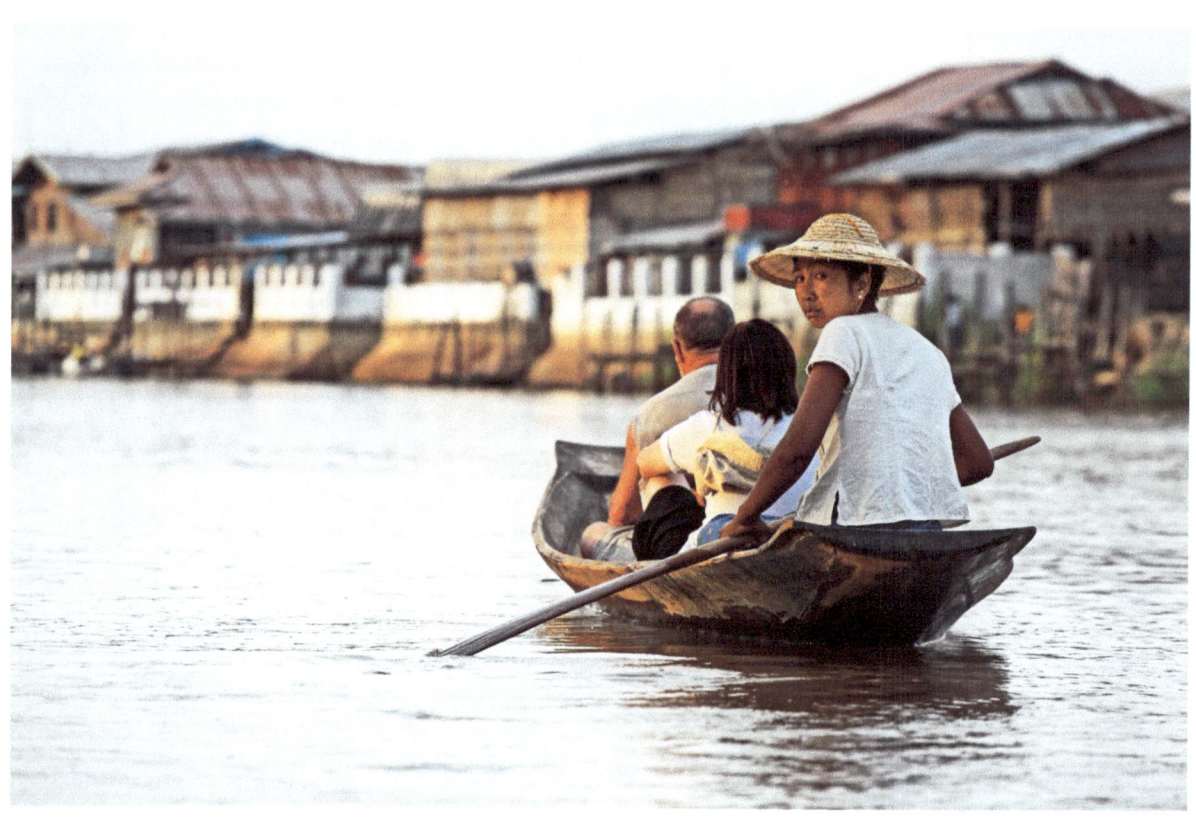

Boatlady ferrying tourists around lake, Nyaung Shwe, Inle Lake, 2009

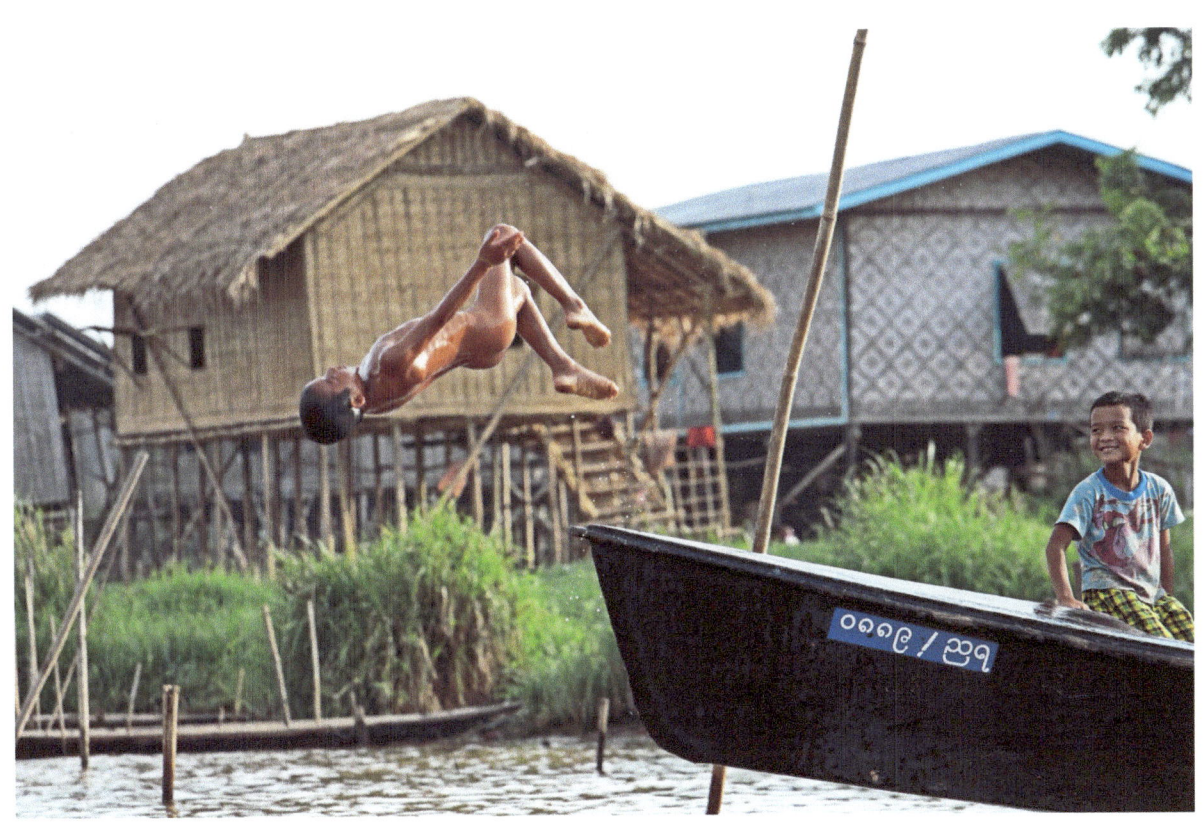

Young boy somersaulting from boat, Nyaung Shwe, Inle Lake, 2009

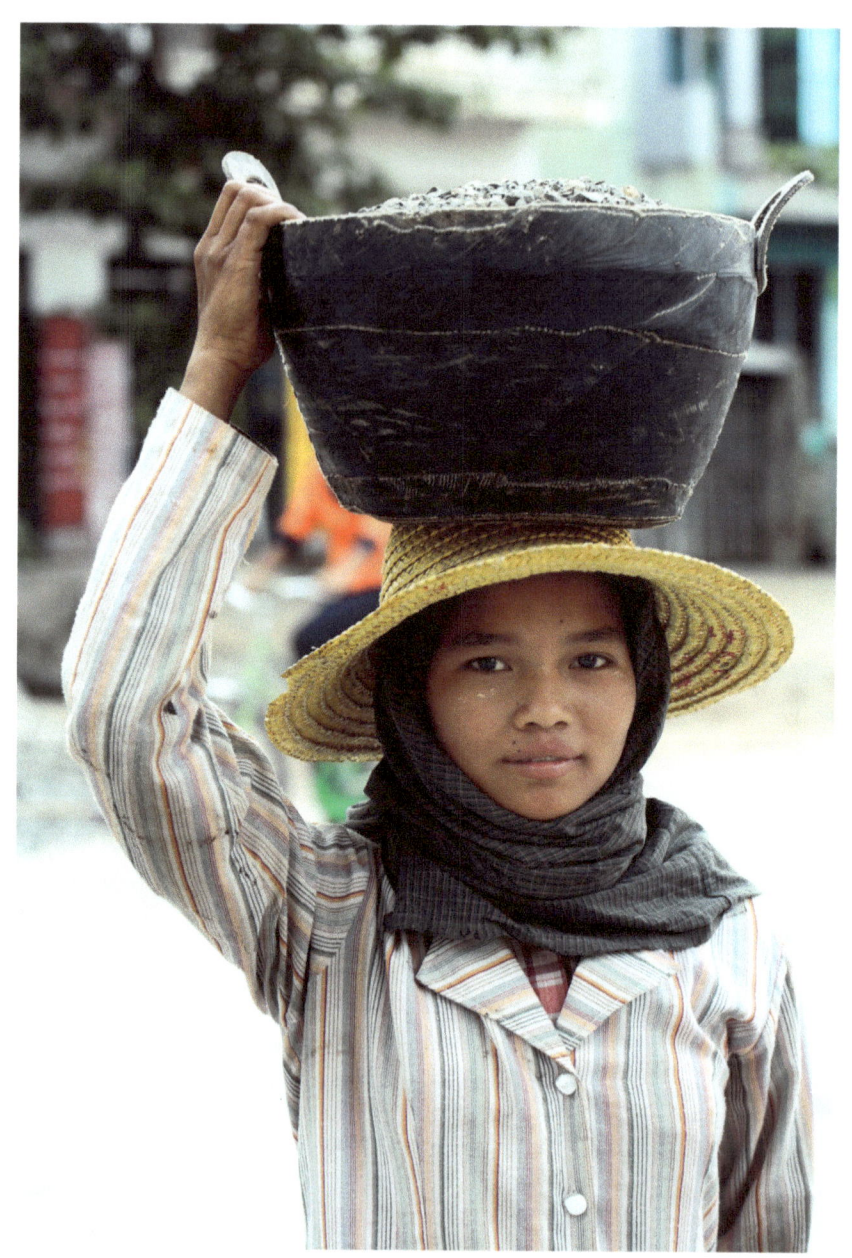

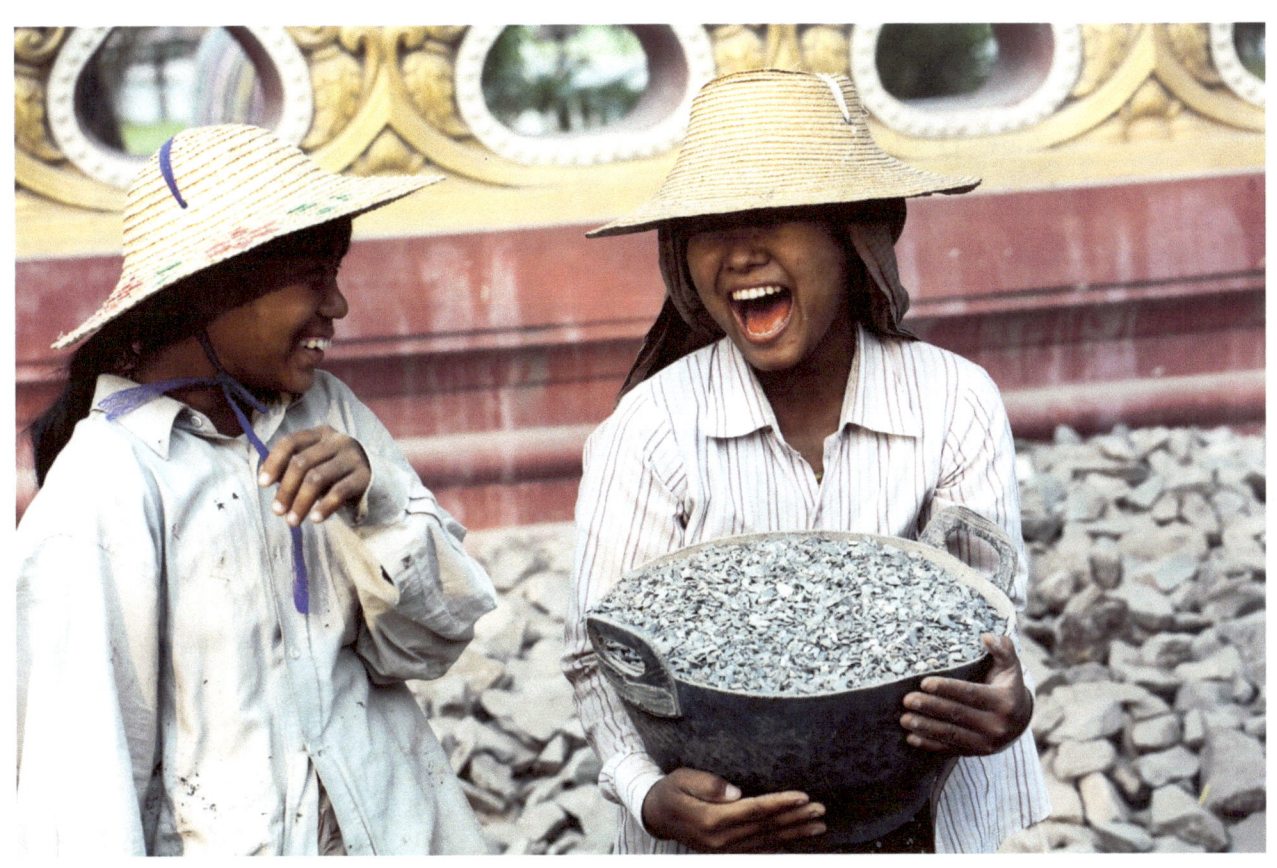

Manual labourers working on roads, Monywa, 2009

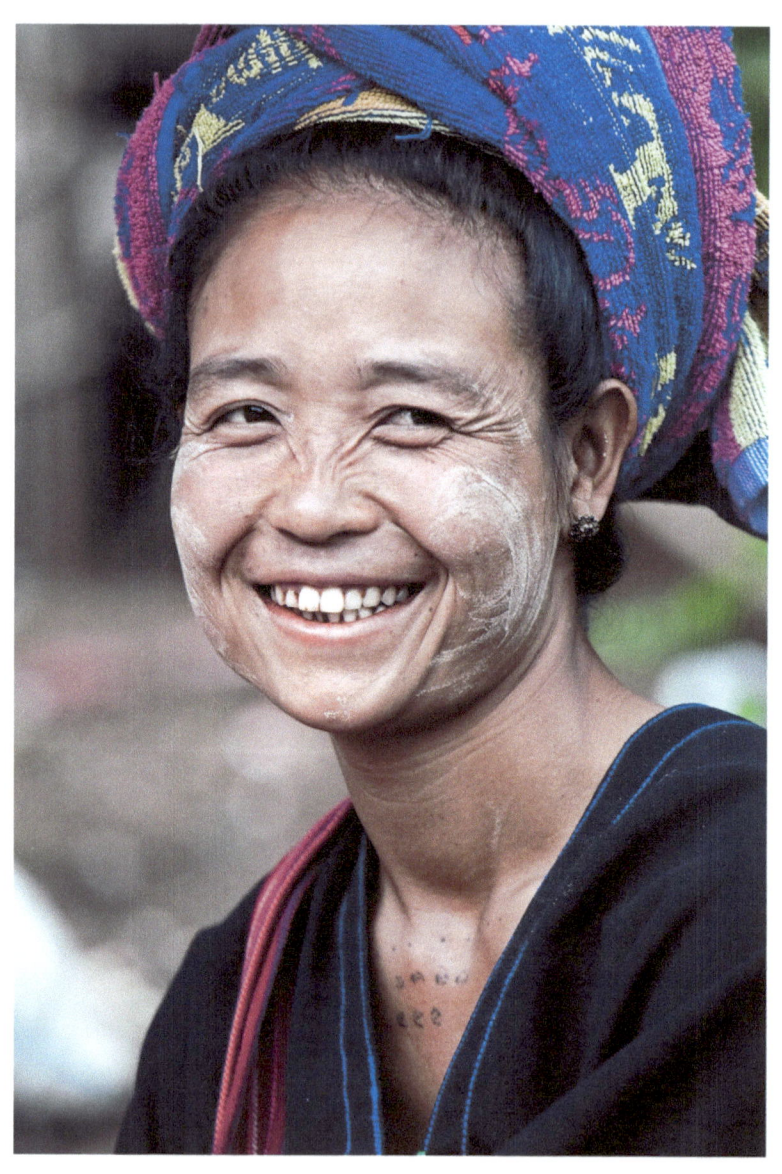

Market Traders at Inle Lake, 2009 in Kalaw (above) & Maing Thauk (right)

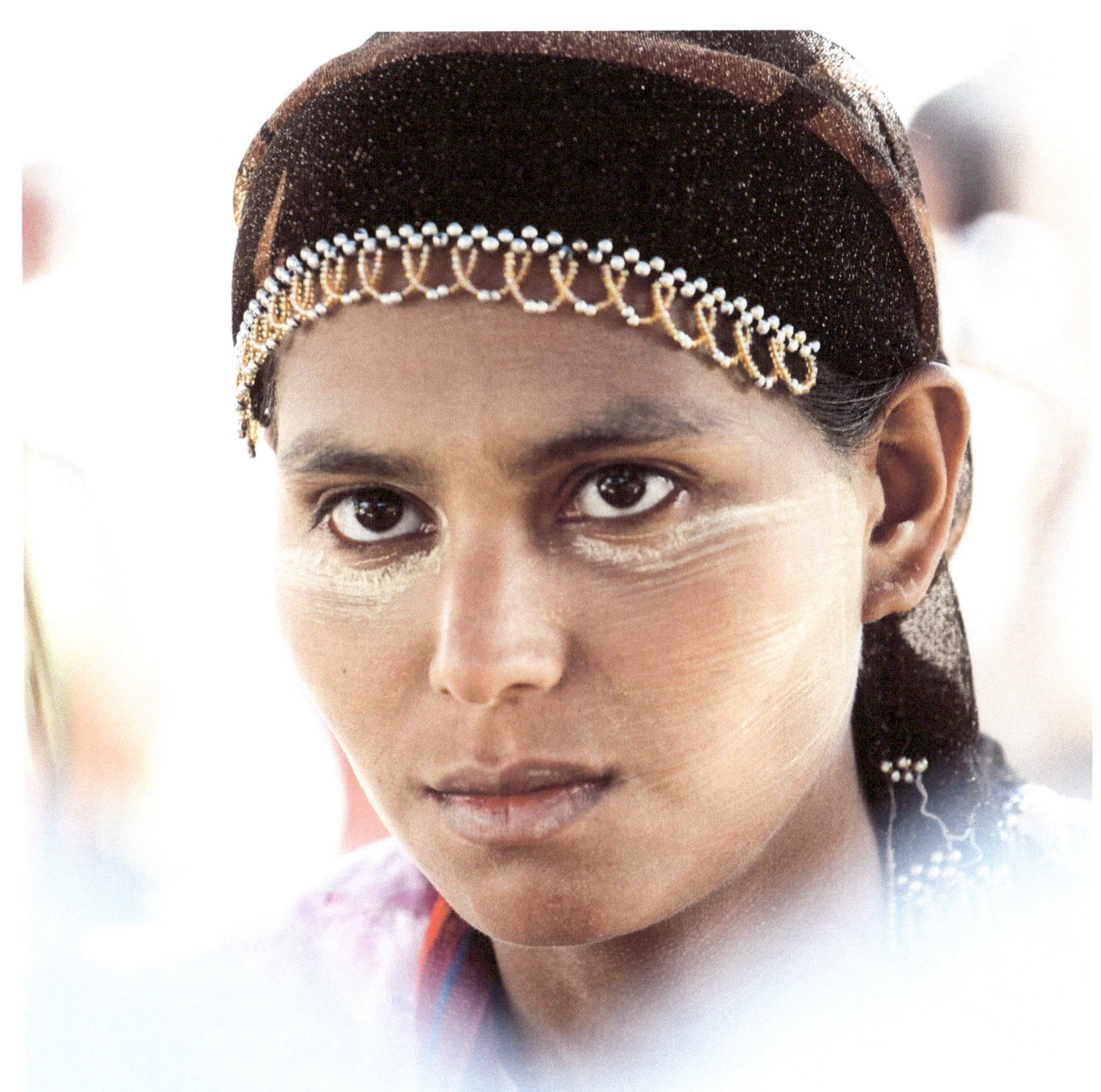

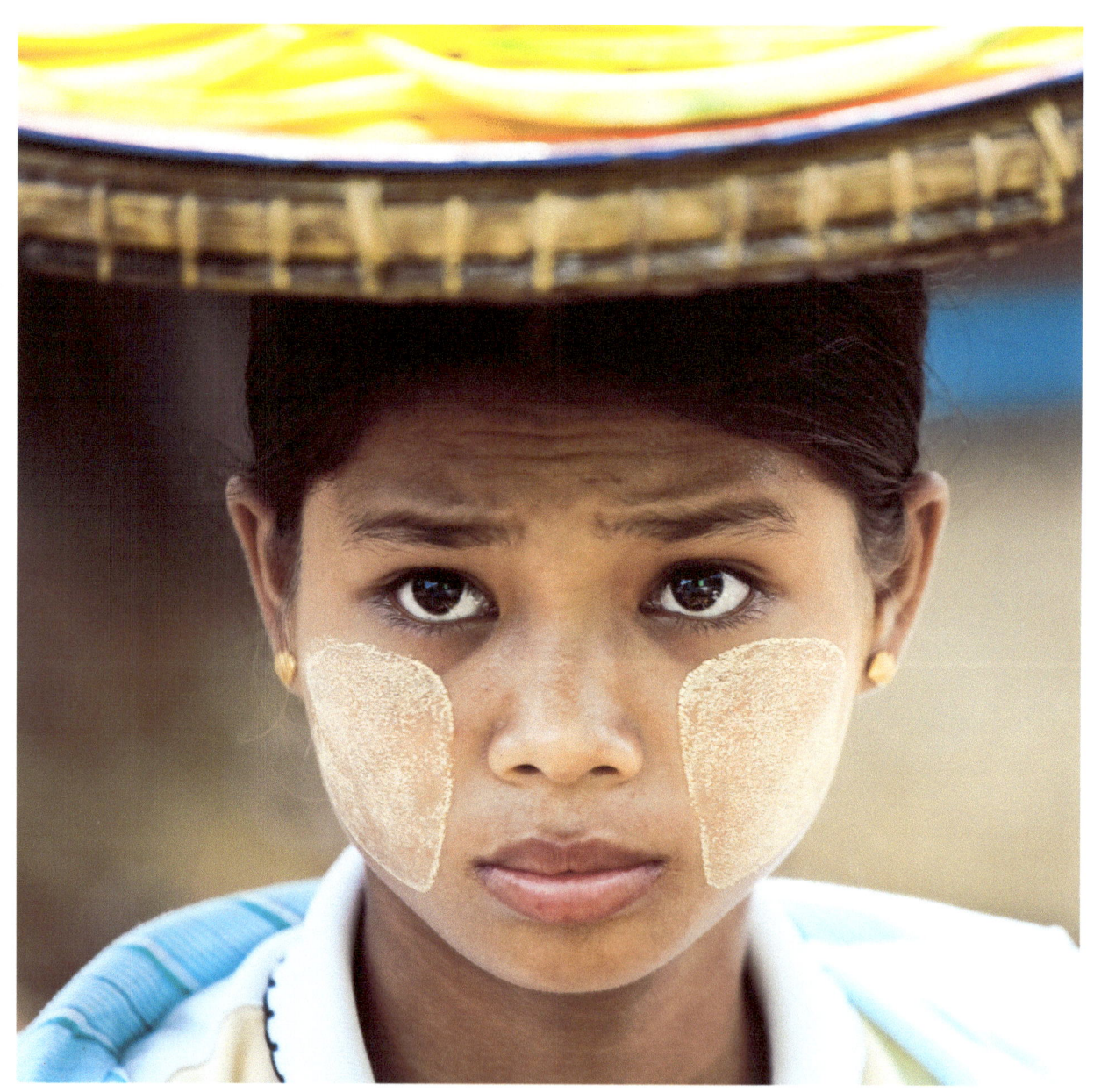

Hawker at Bus Stand, Magwe, 2009

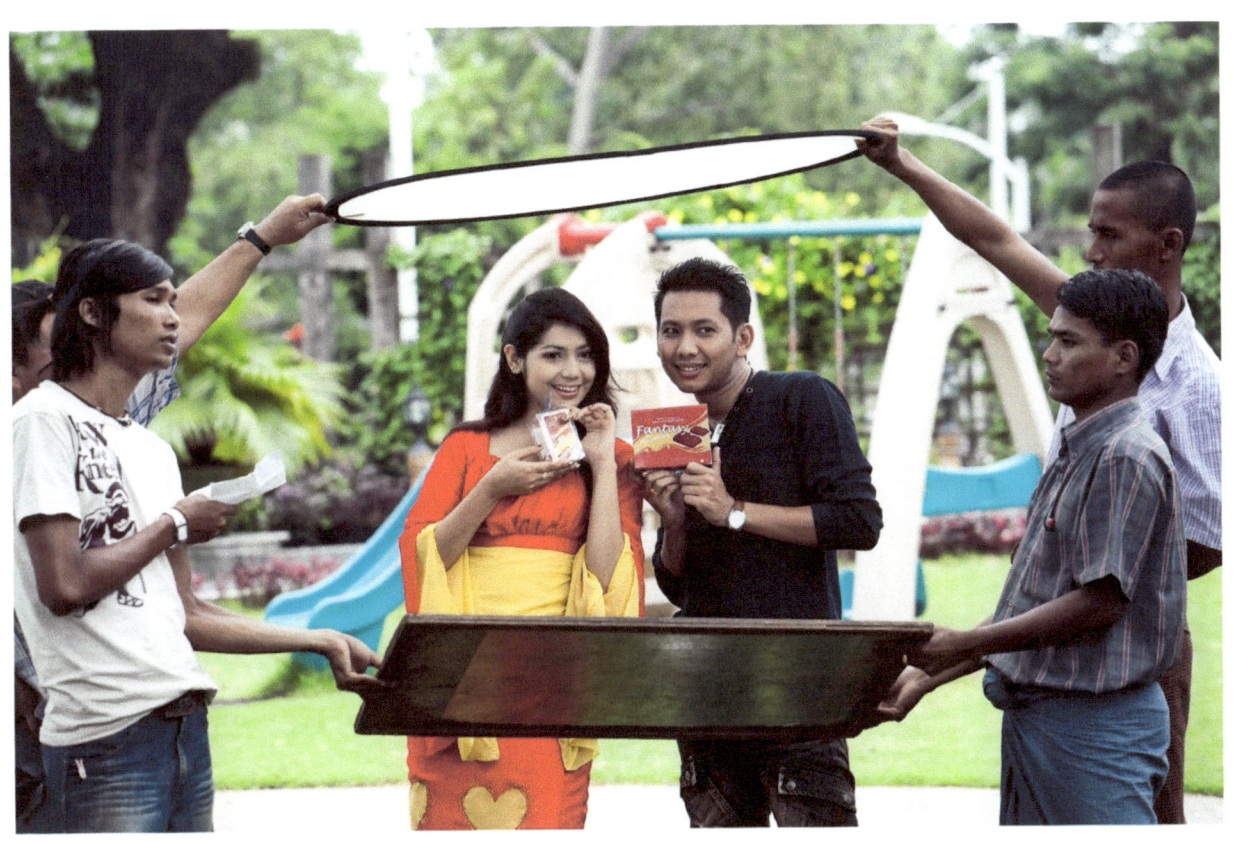

Actors filming advert in park, Yangon, 2009

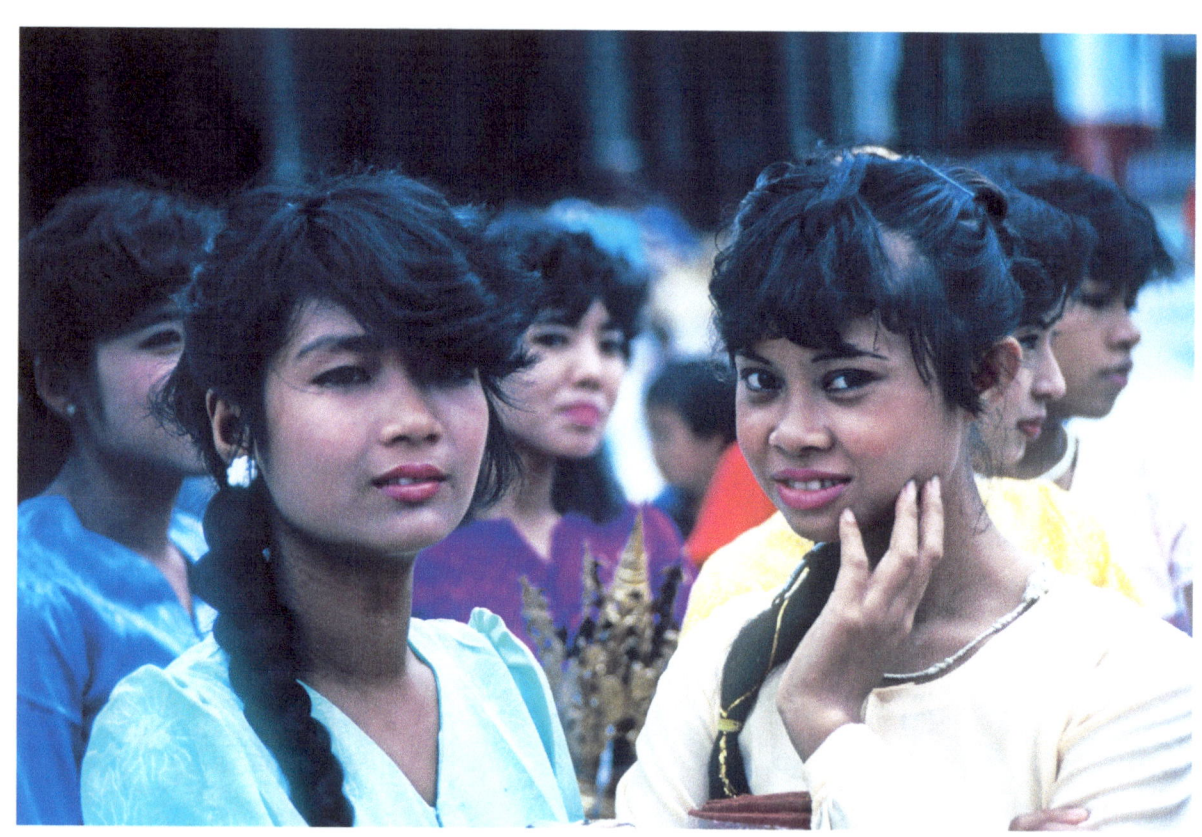

Young females at Shwedagon Pagoda, Yangon, 1988

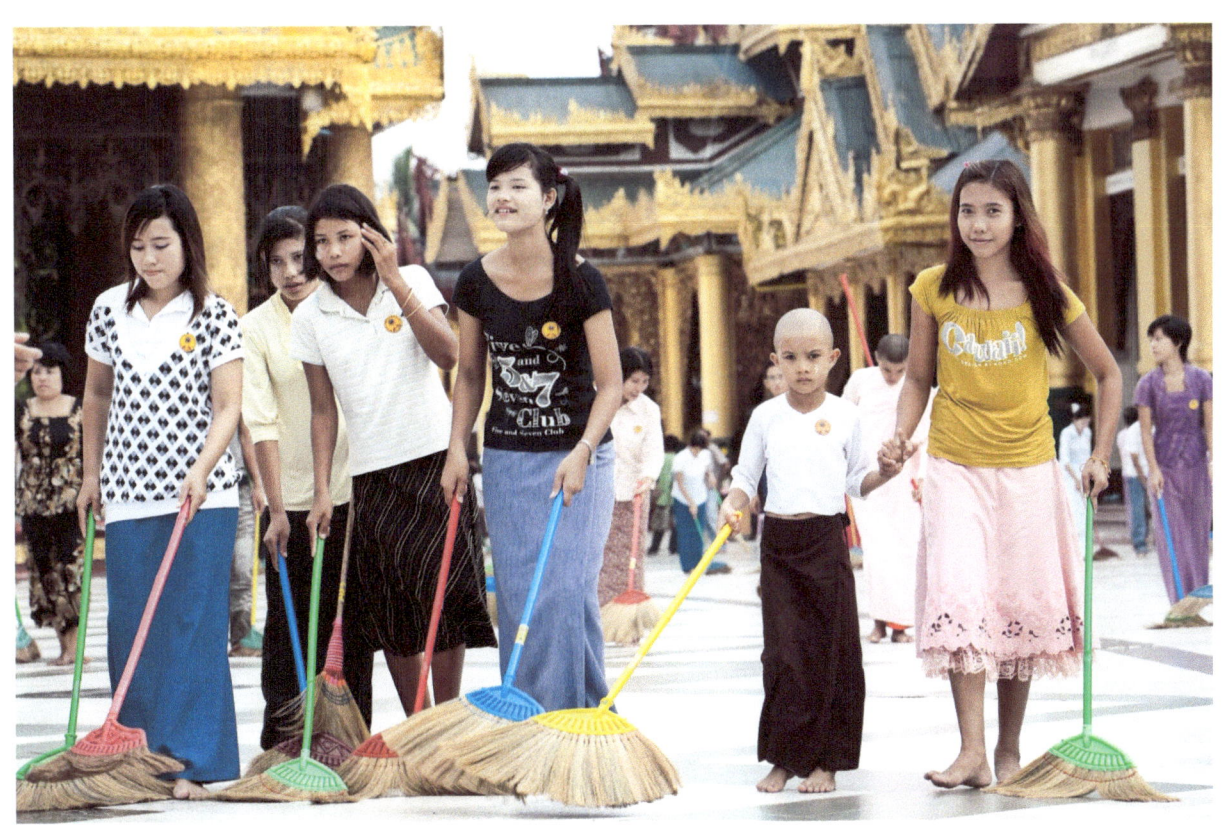

Sweeping Temple floor to gain merit, Shwedagon Pagoda, 2009

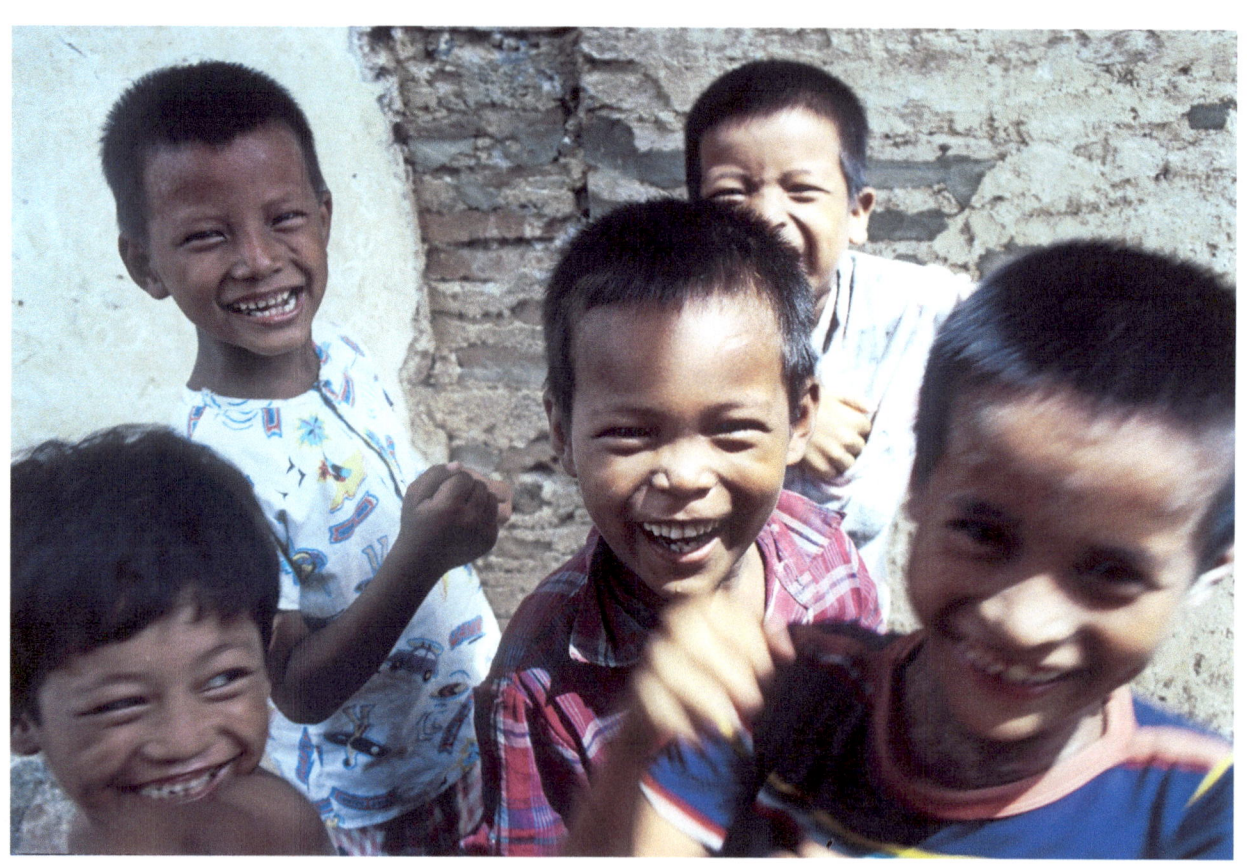

Young boys play acting in street, Mandalay, 1988

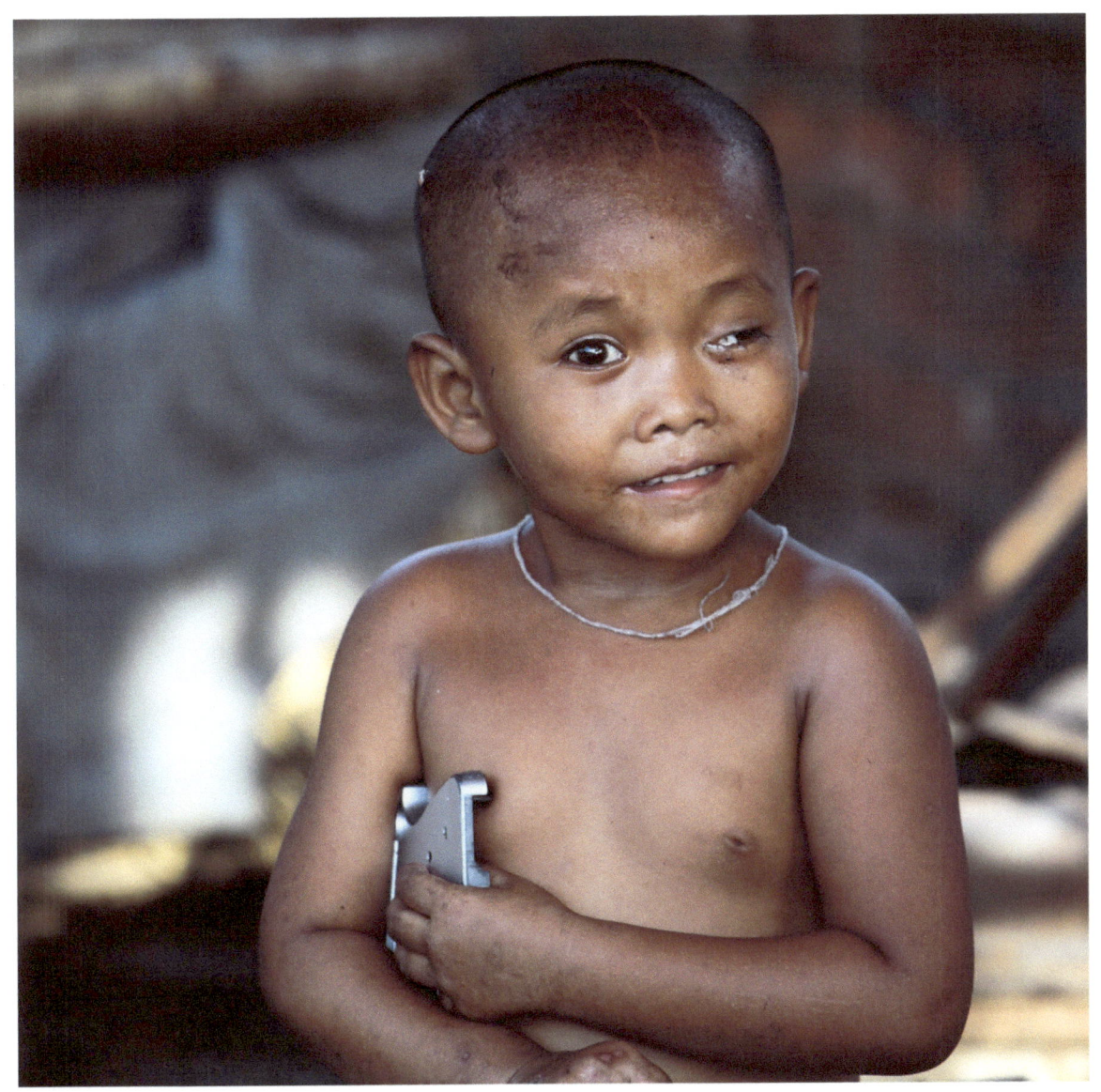

Young boy with cataract, Mandalay, 2009

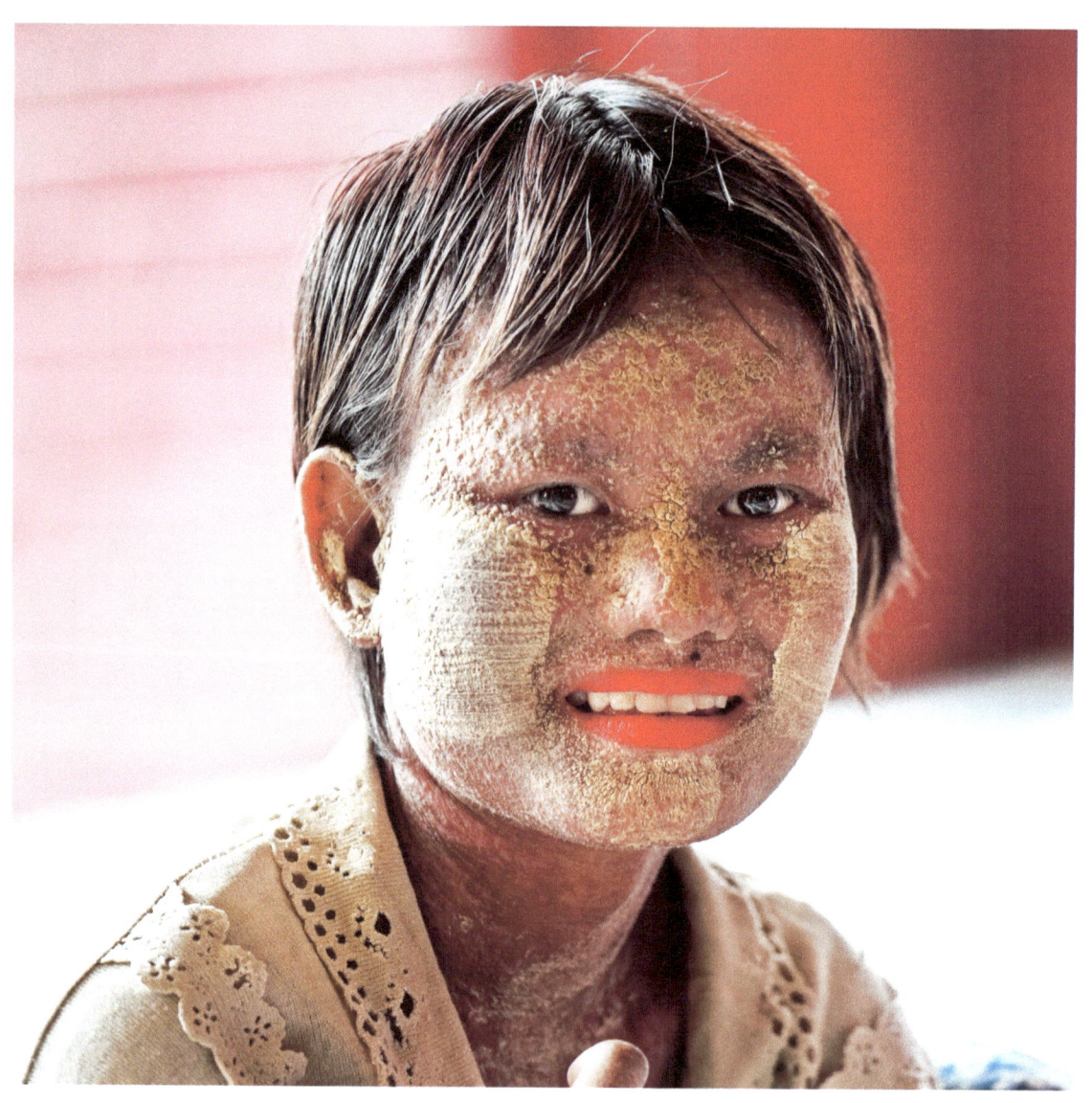

Young female at Mahamuni Paya, Mandalay, 2009

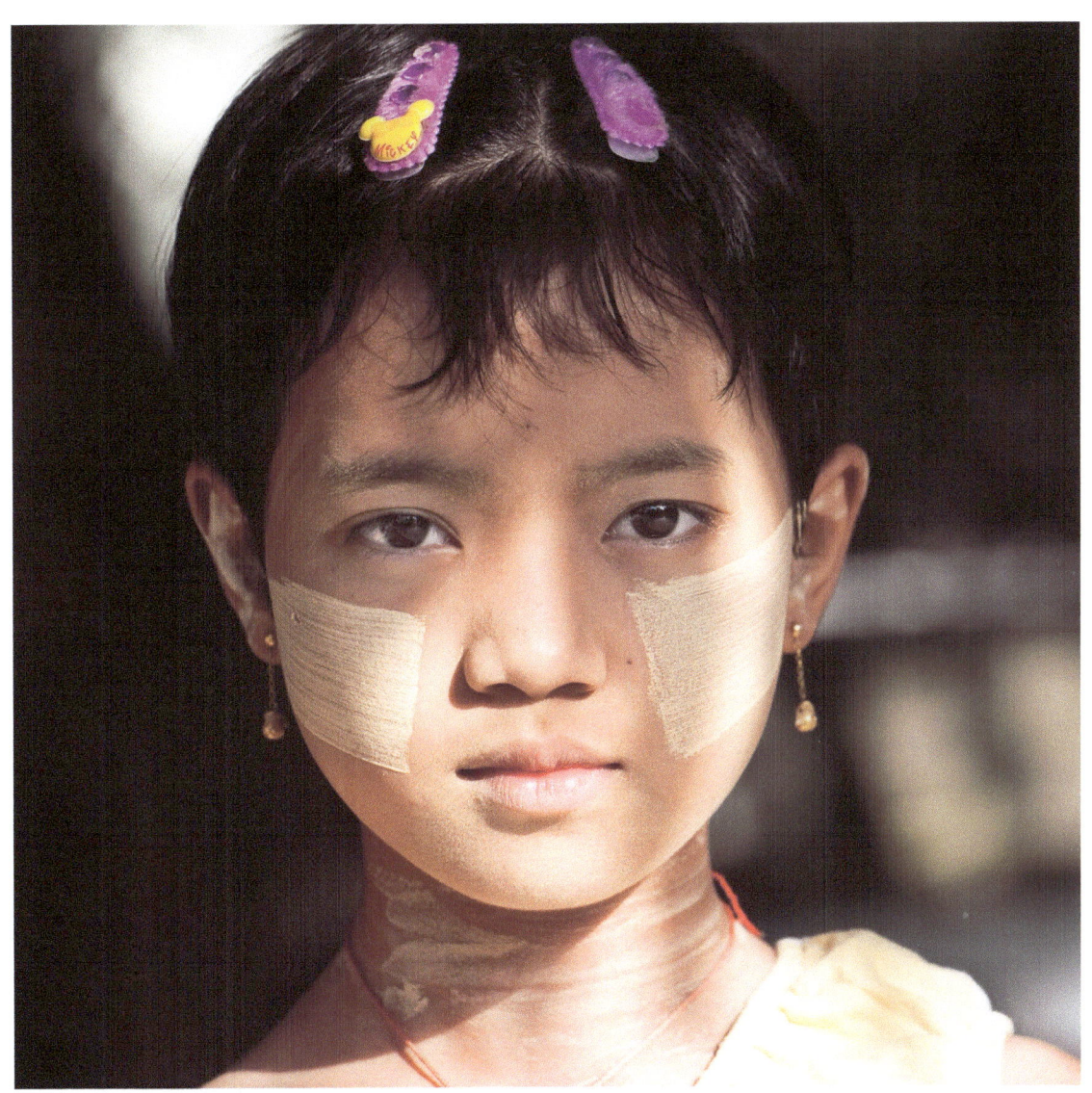

Young female in street, Mandalay, 2009

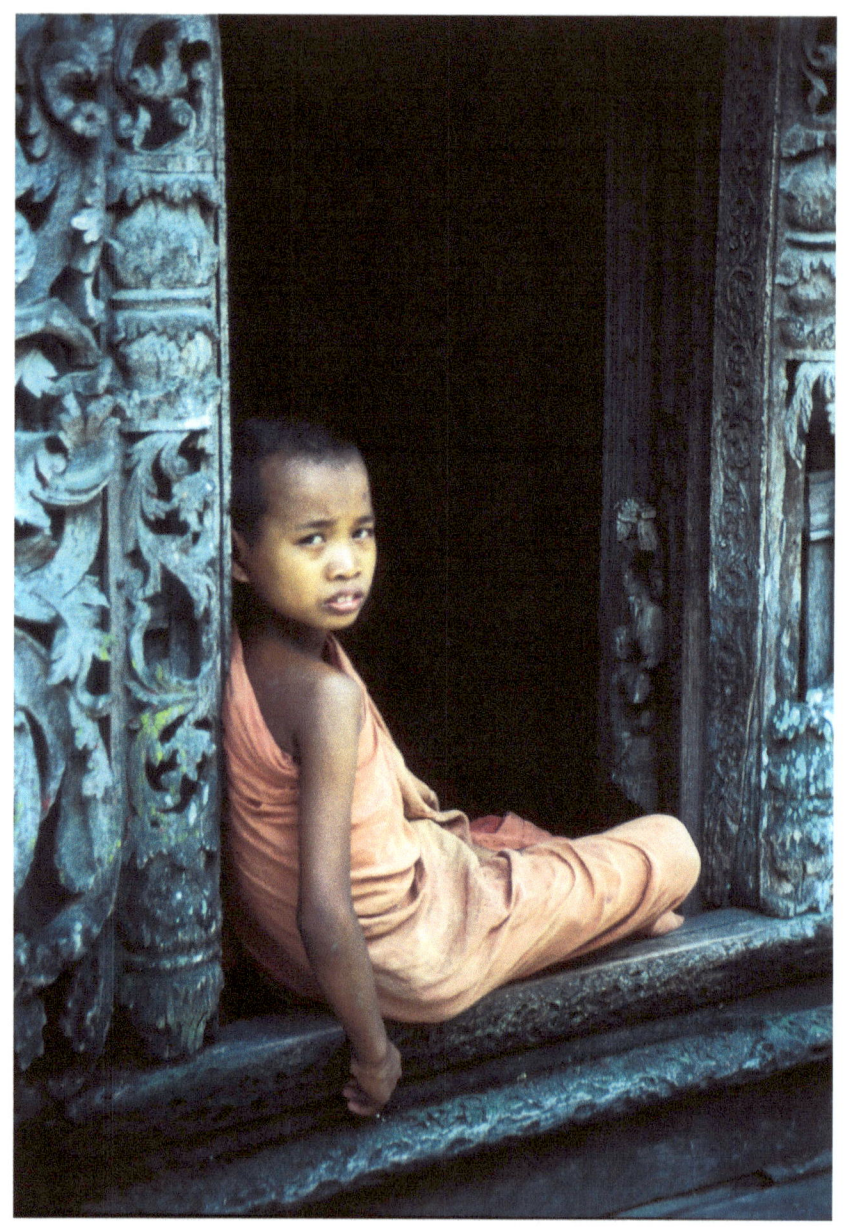

Novice Monk in Temple doorway, Bagan, 1988

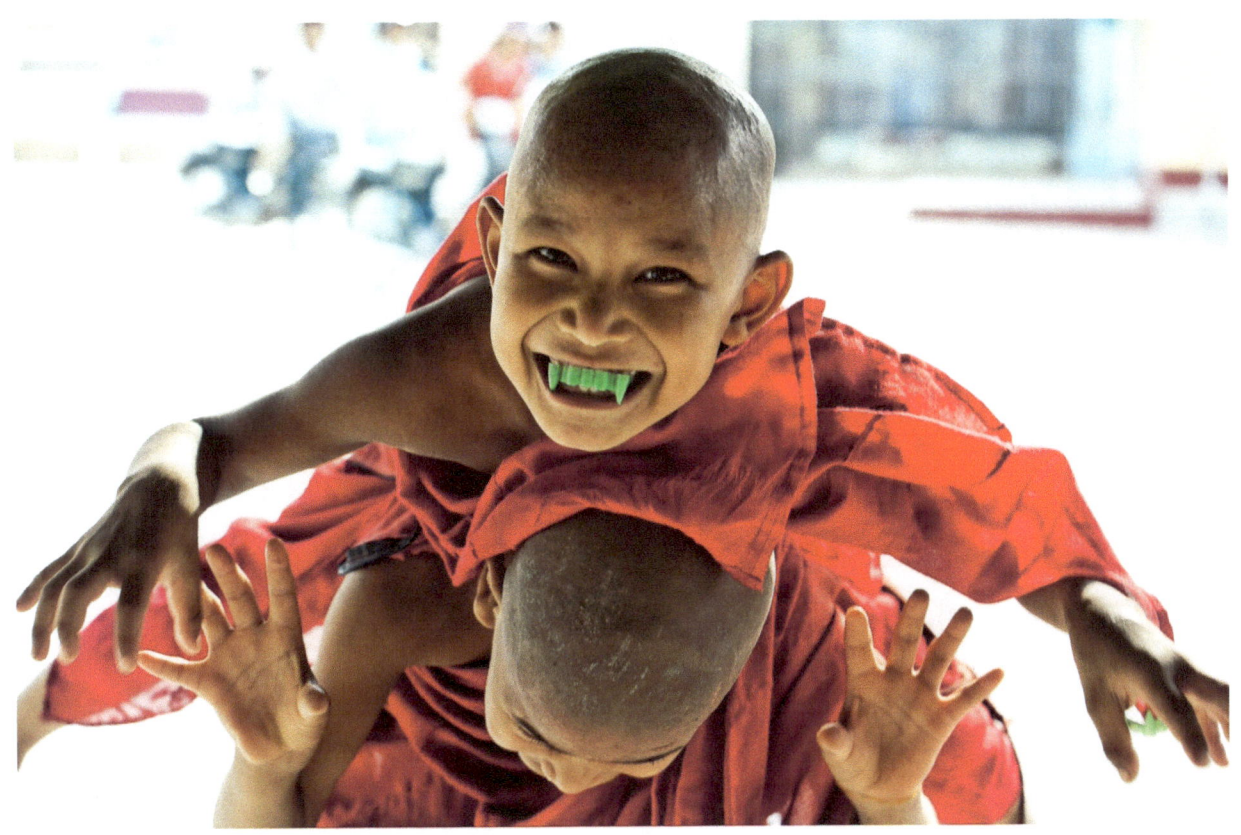

Novice monk with Dracula fangs, Thanboddhay Paya, Monywa, 2009

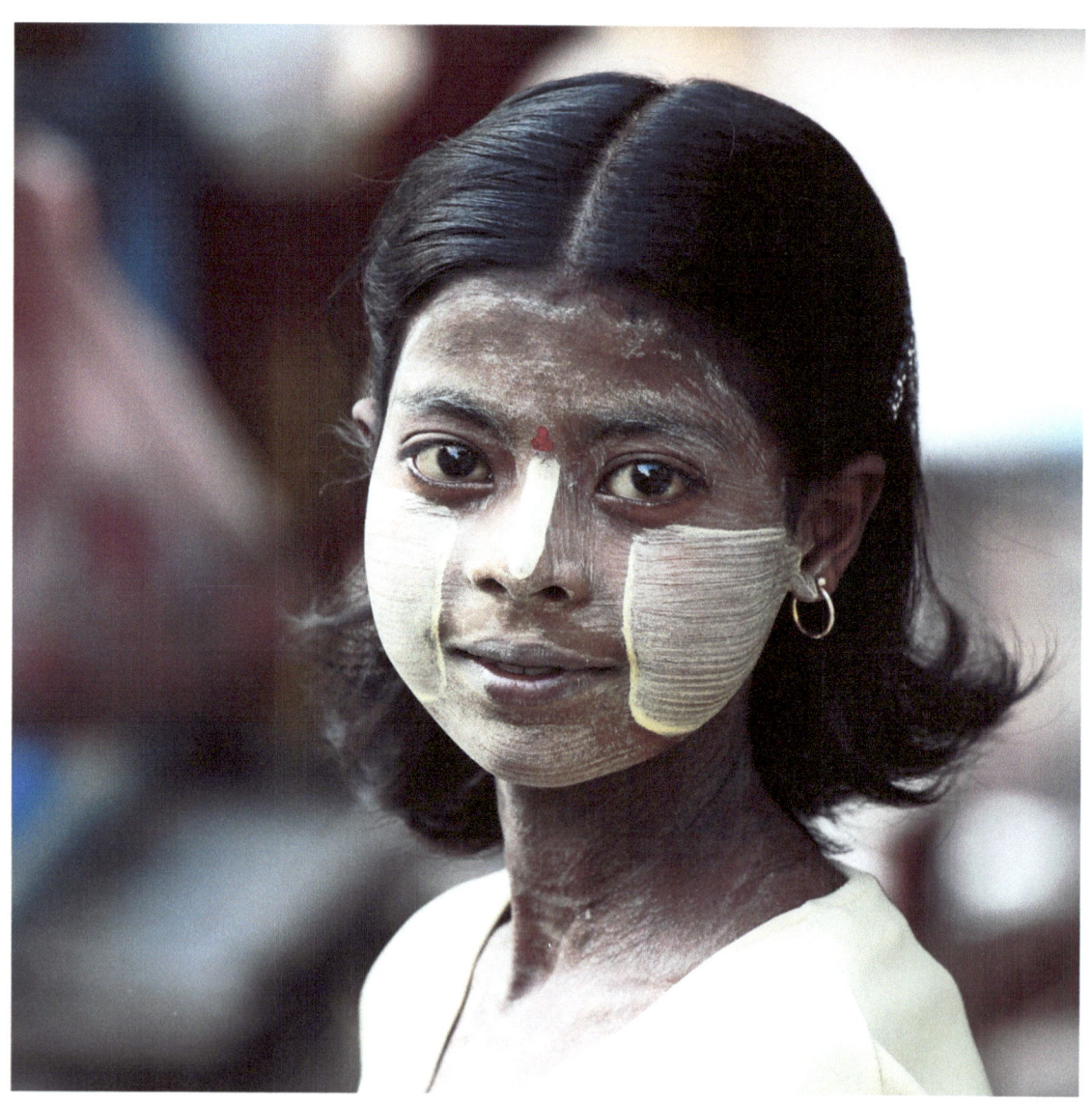

Young girl outside Hindu Temple, Mandalay, 2009

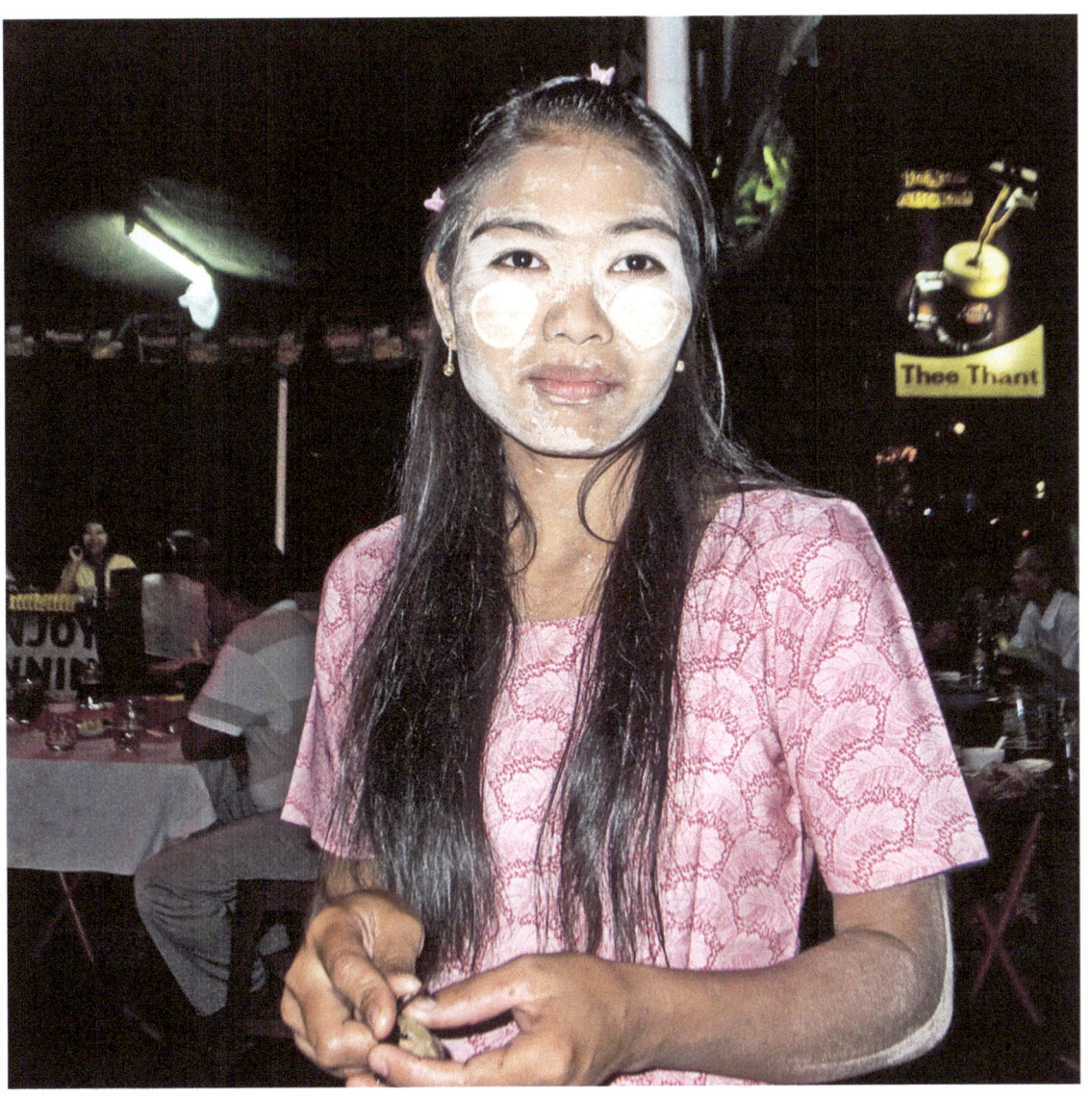

Restaurant Waitress, Pyay, 2009

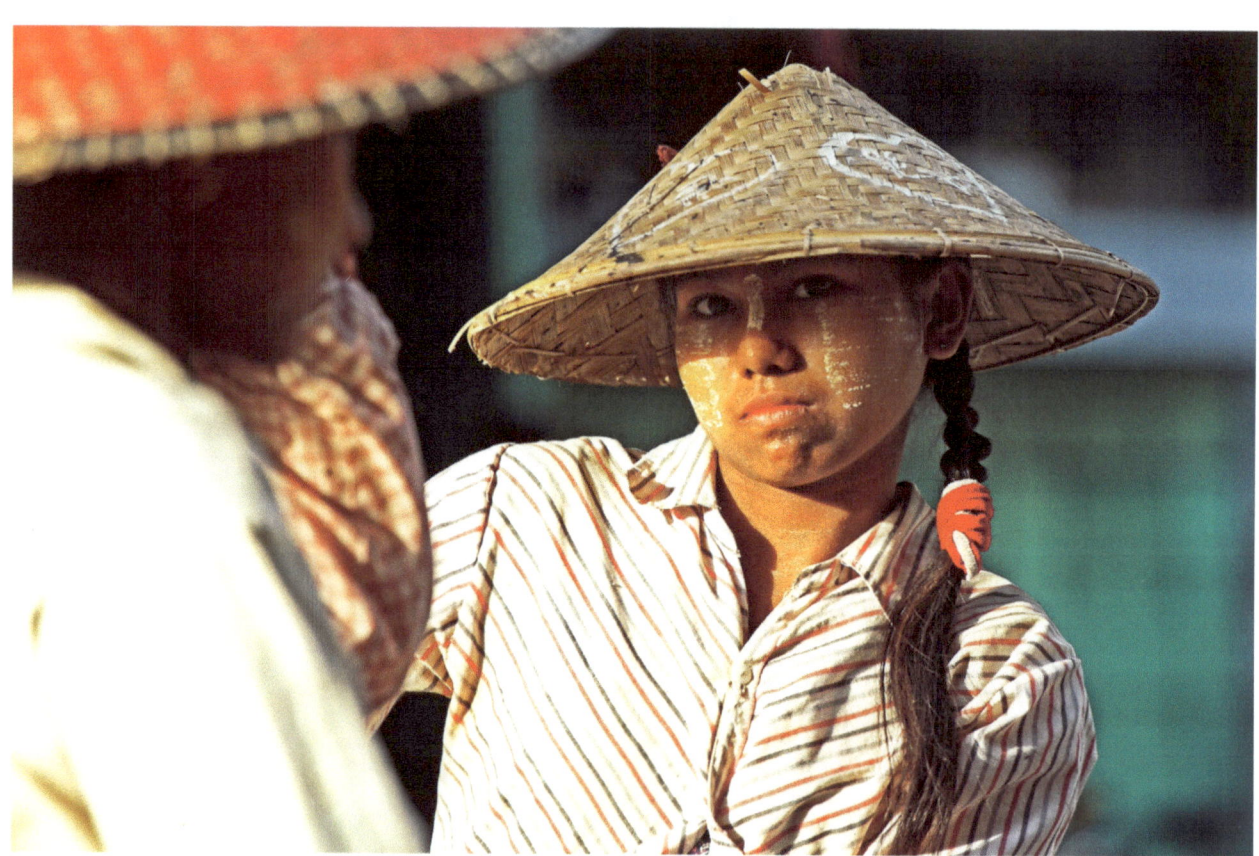

Manual labourers working on roads, Mandalay, 2009

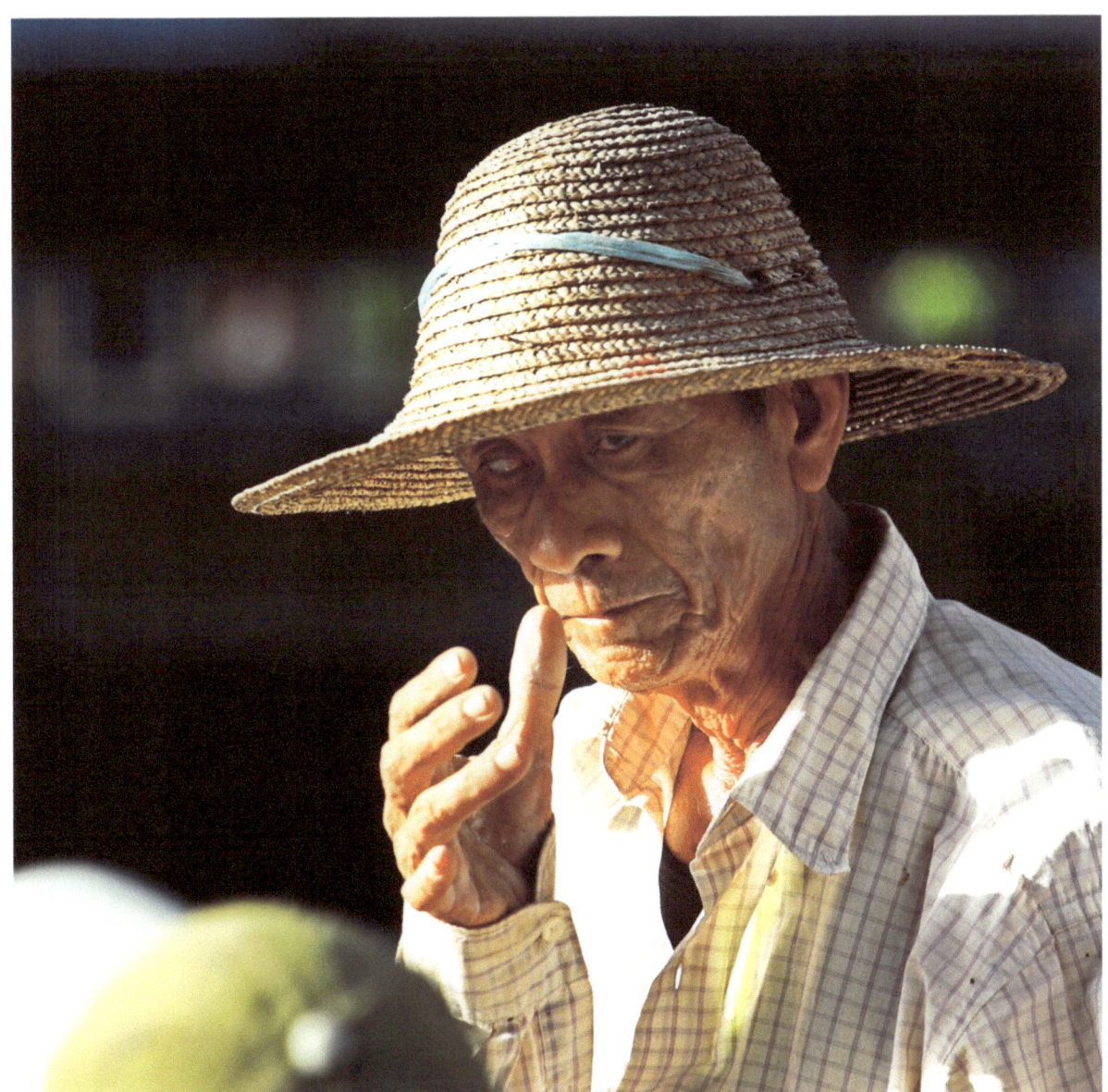

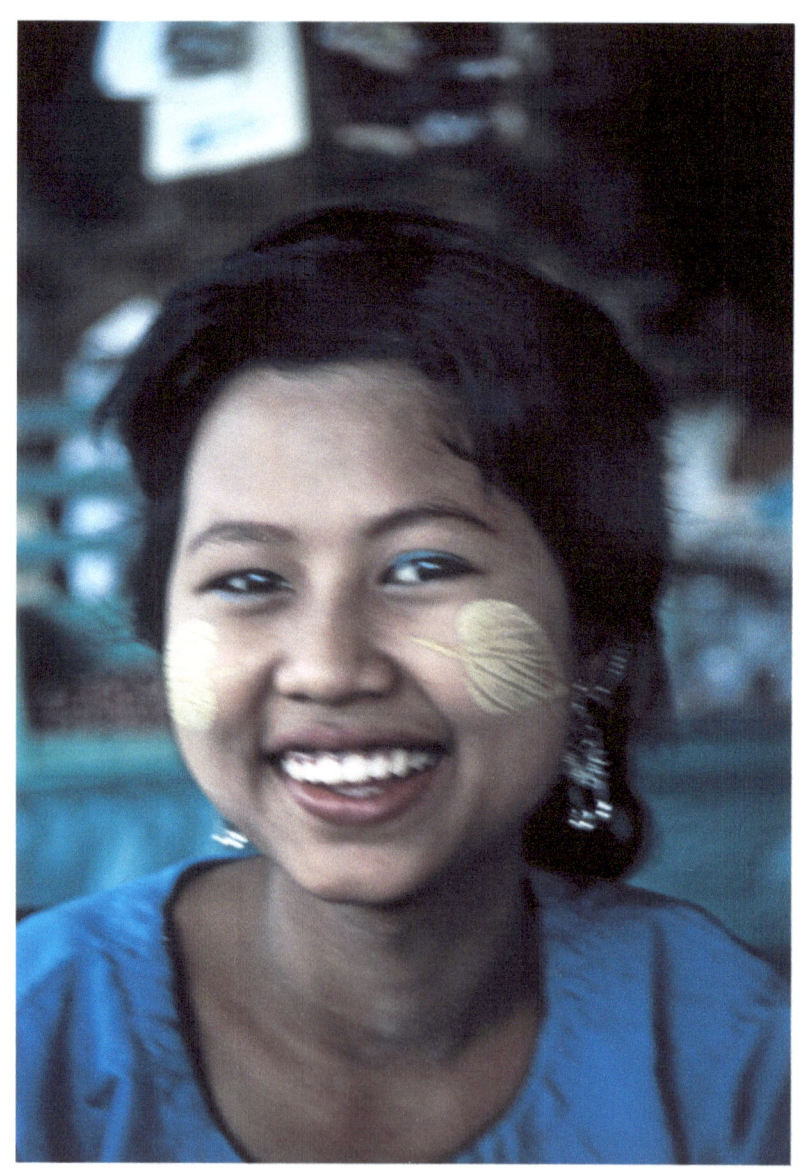

"Amy", Bagan, 1988

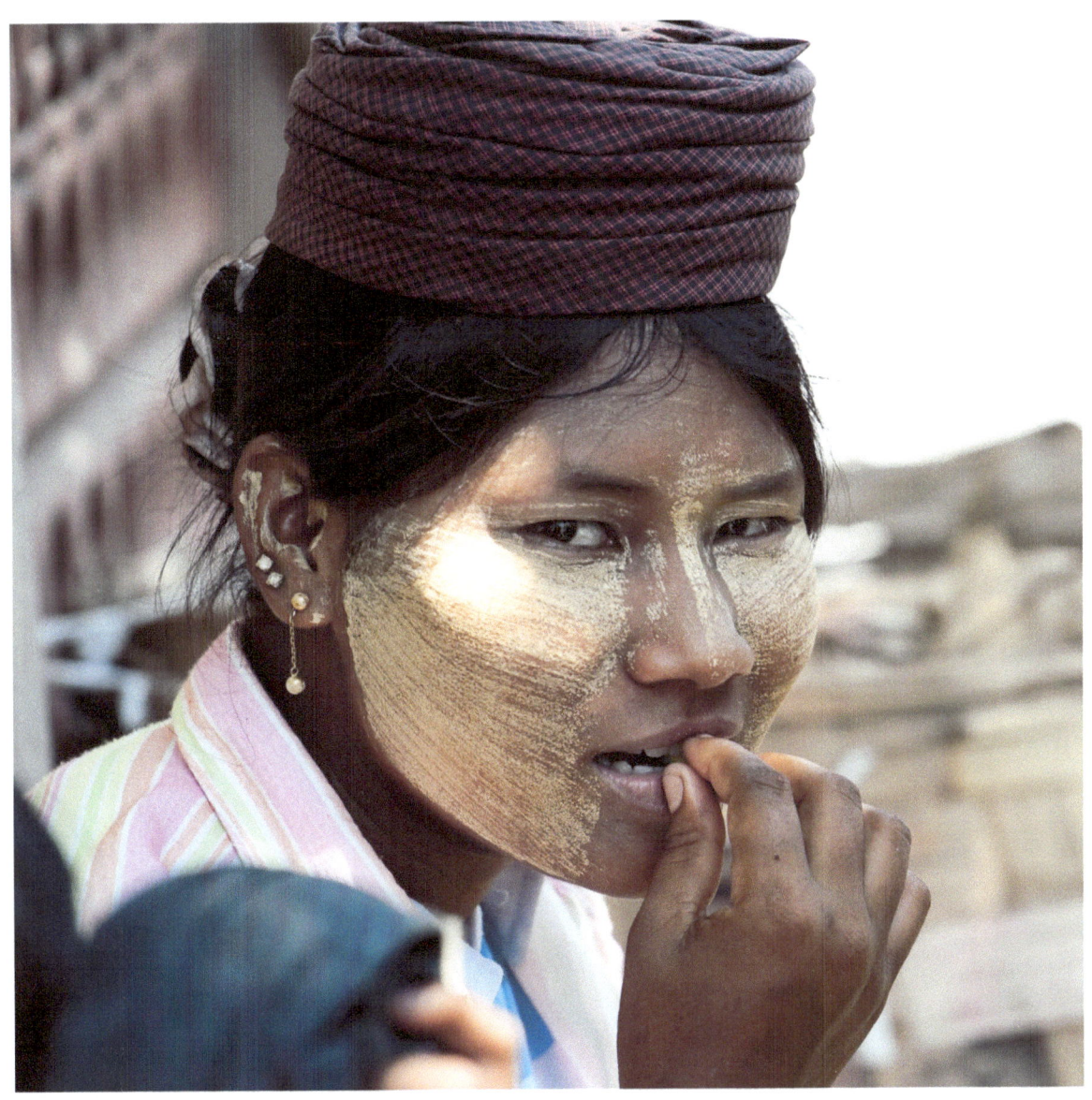

Hawker at Bus Stand, Monywa, 2009

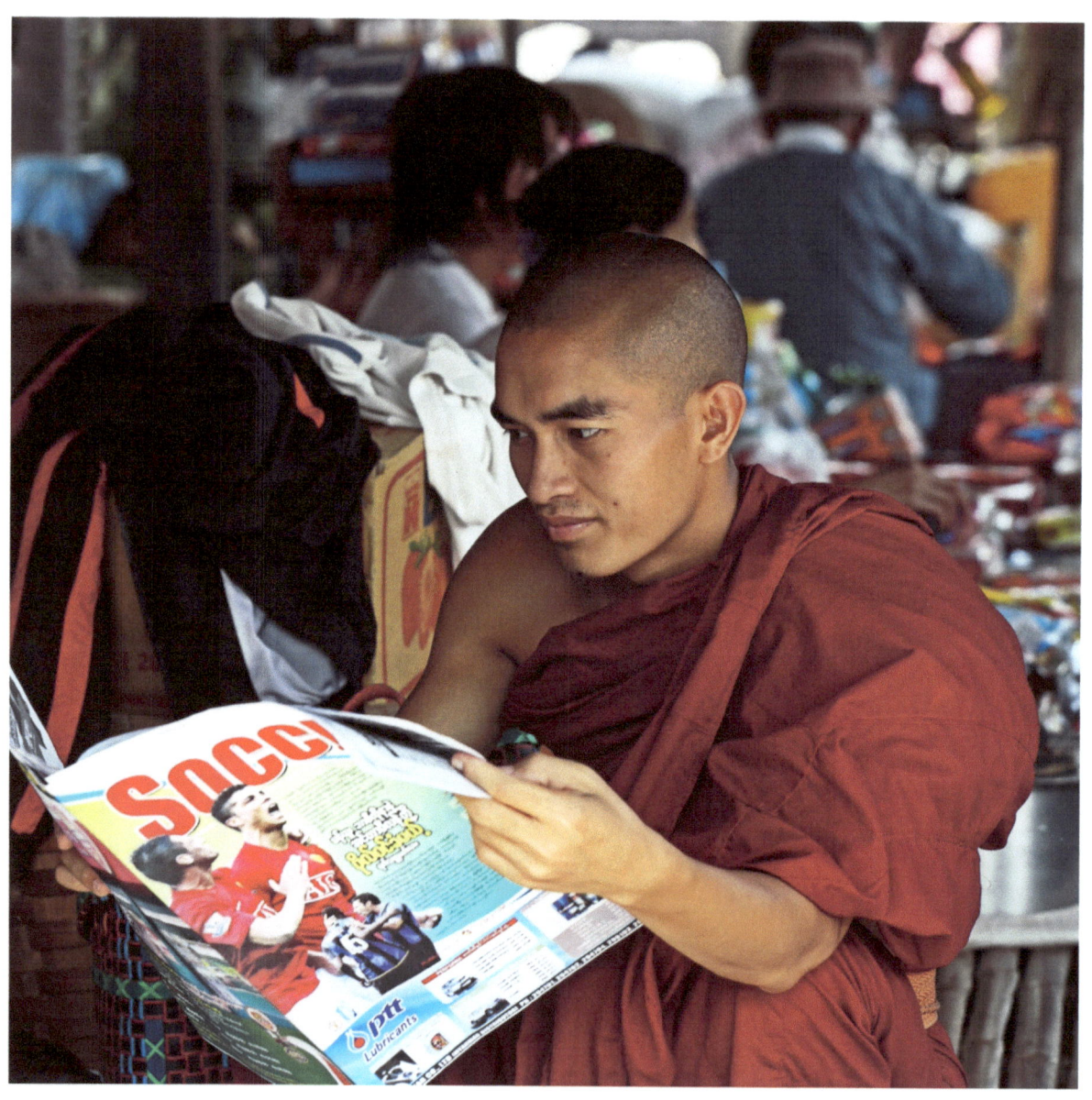

Monk reading Burmese Soccer Magazine, Maing Thauk, Inle Lake, 2009

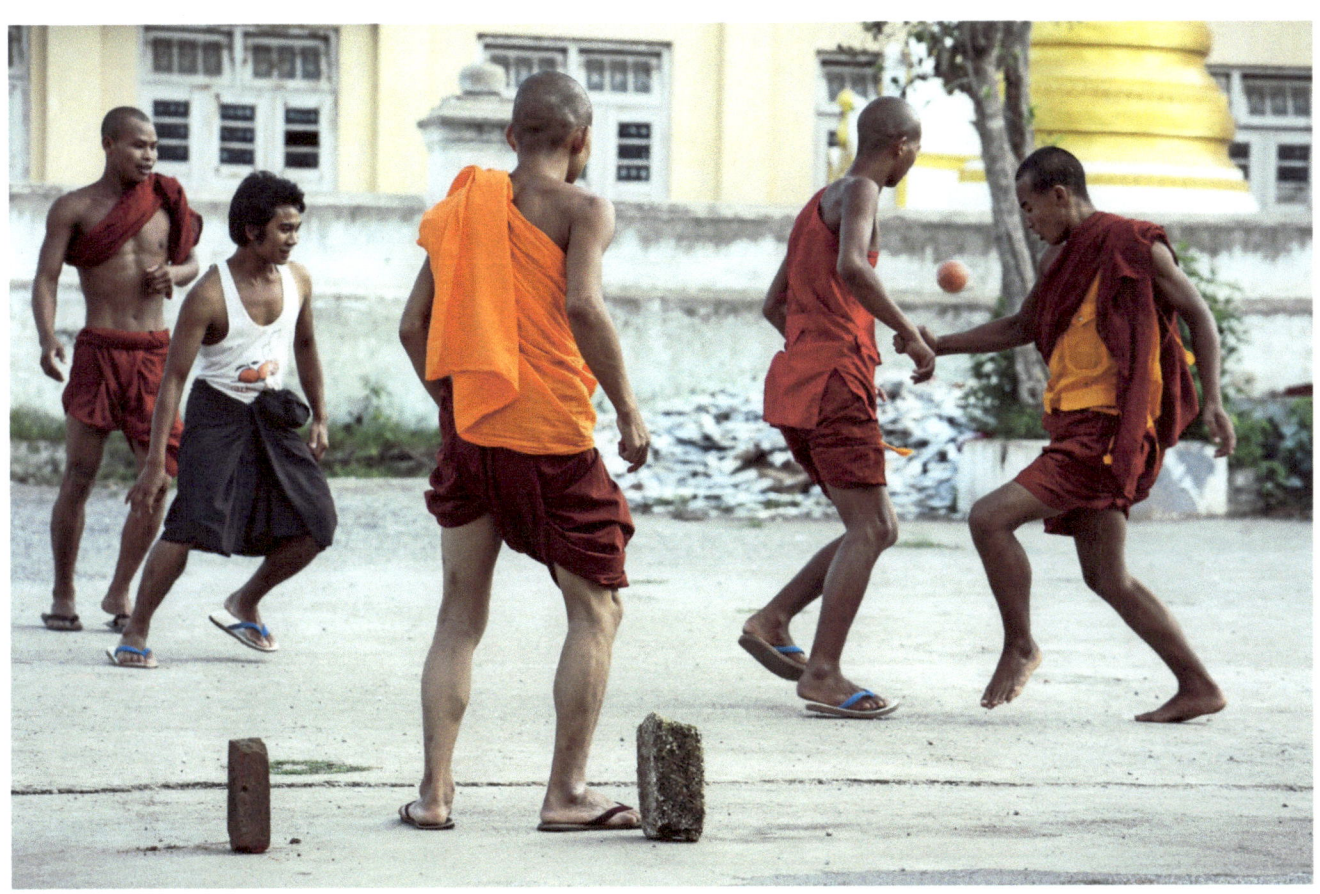

Monks playing football, Kalaw, Inle Lake, 2009

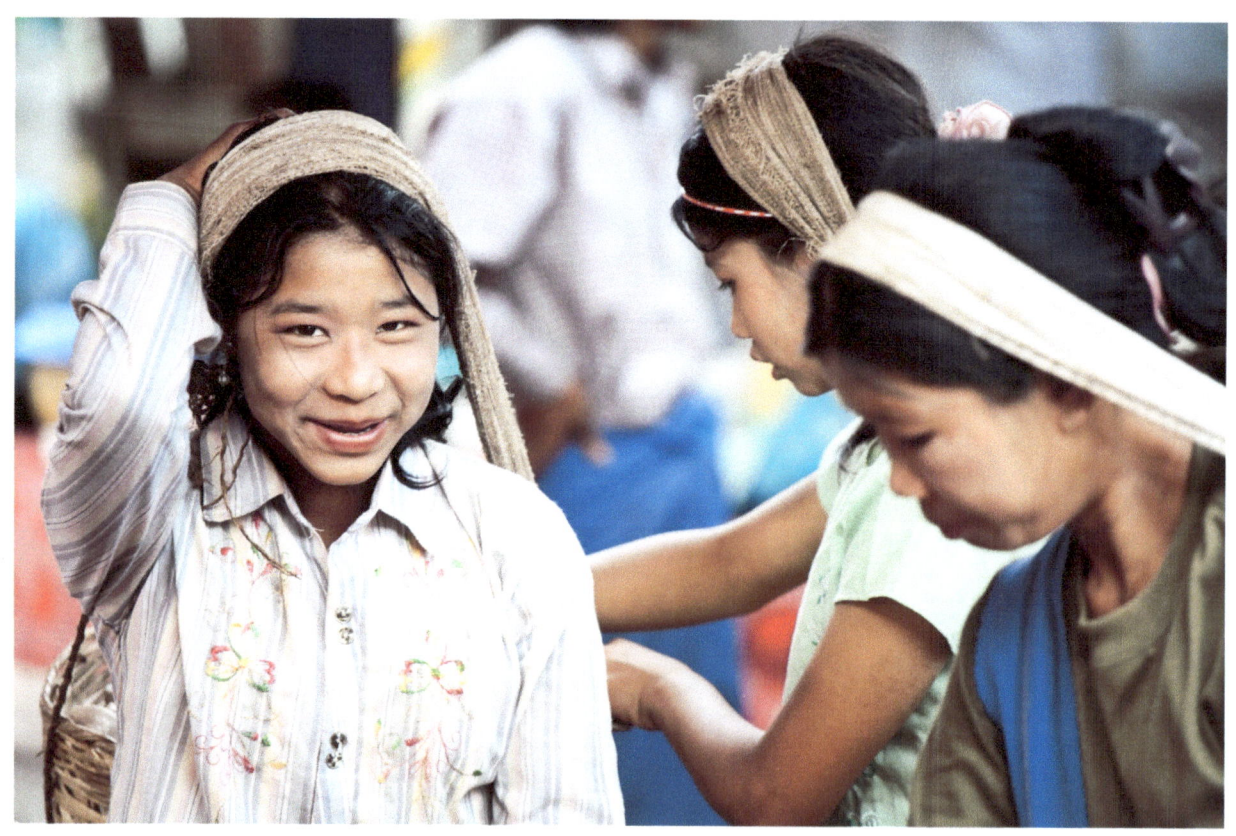

Females shopping at market, Kalaw, Inle Lake, 2009

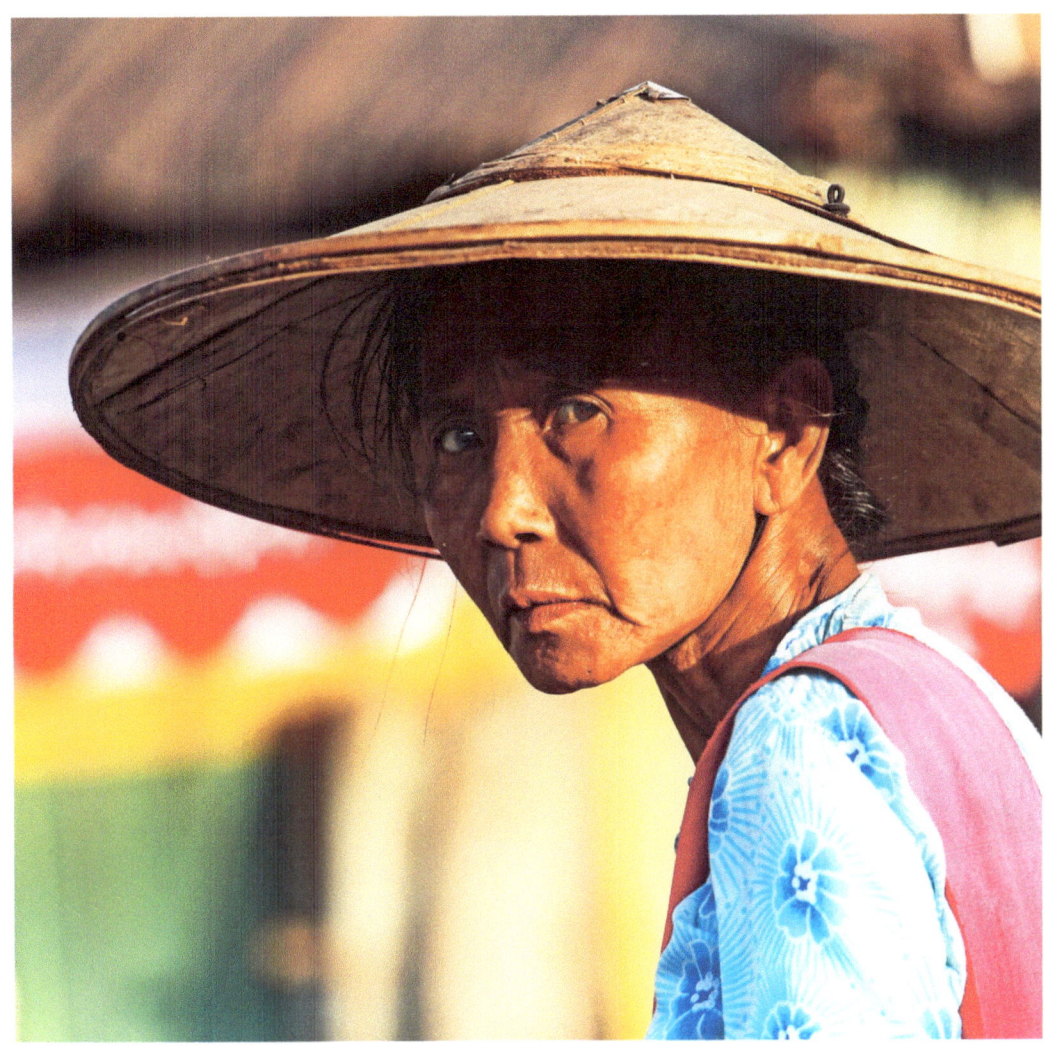

Street Cleaner at sunset, Kalaw, Inle Lake, 2009

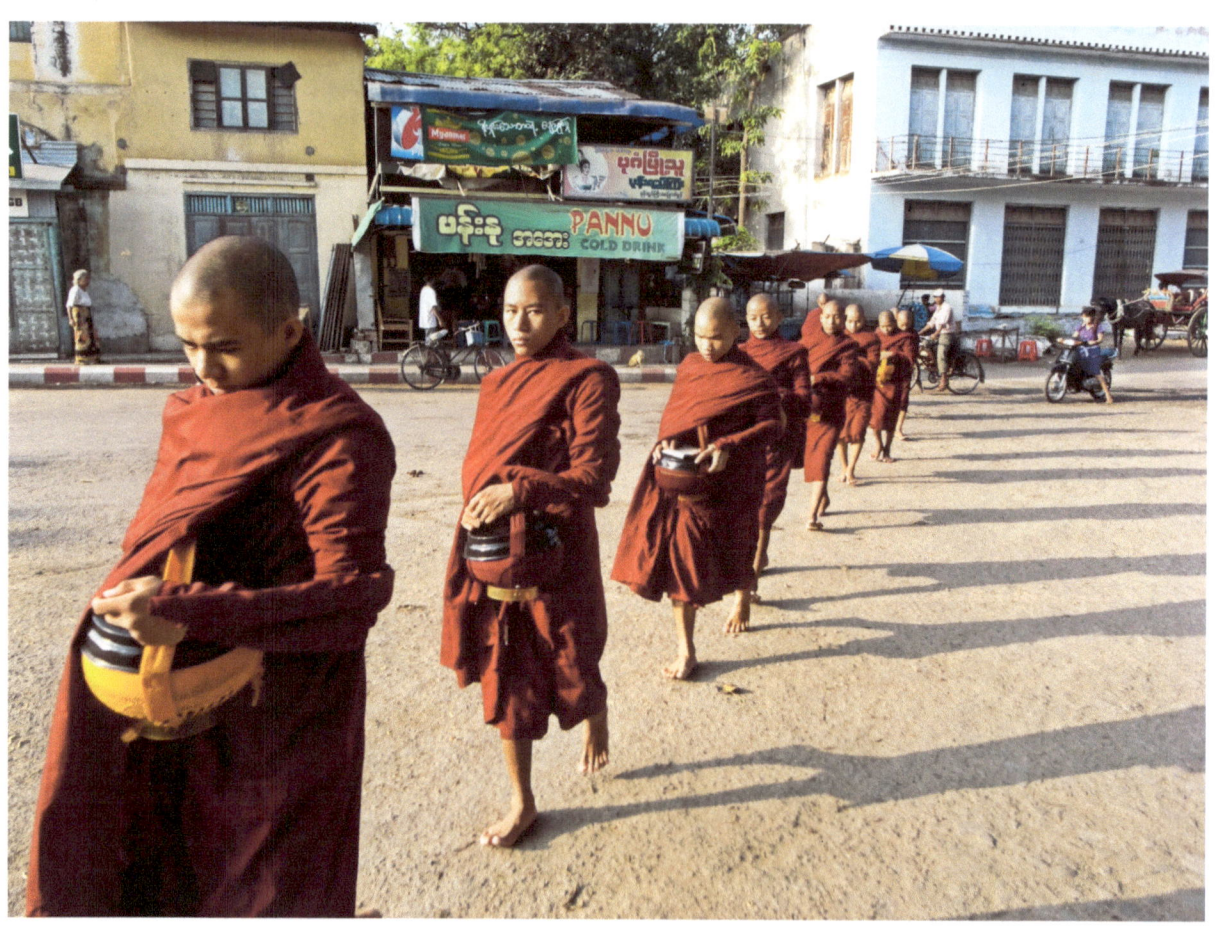

Monks collecting daily food offerings early morning, Bagan, 2009

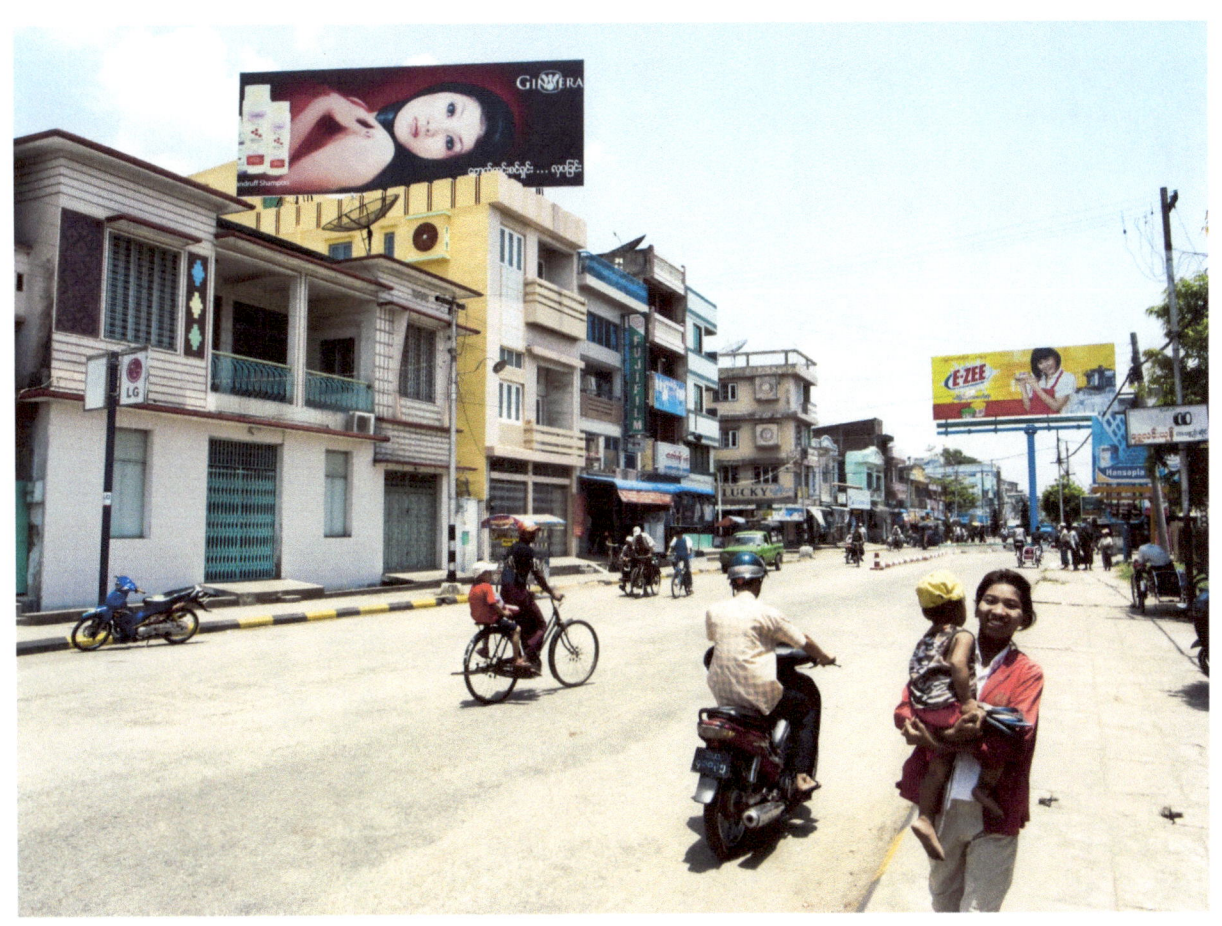

High Street, Pyay, 2009

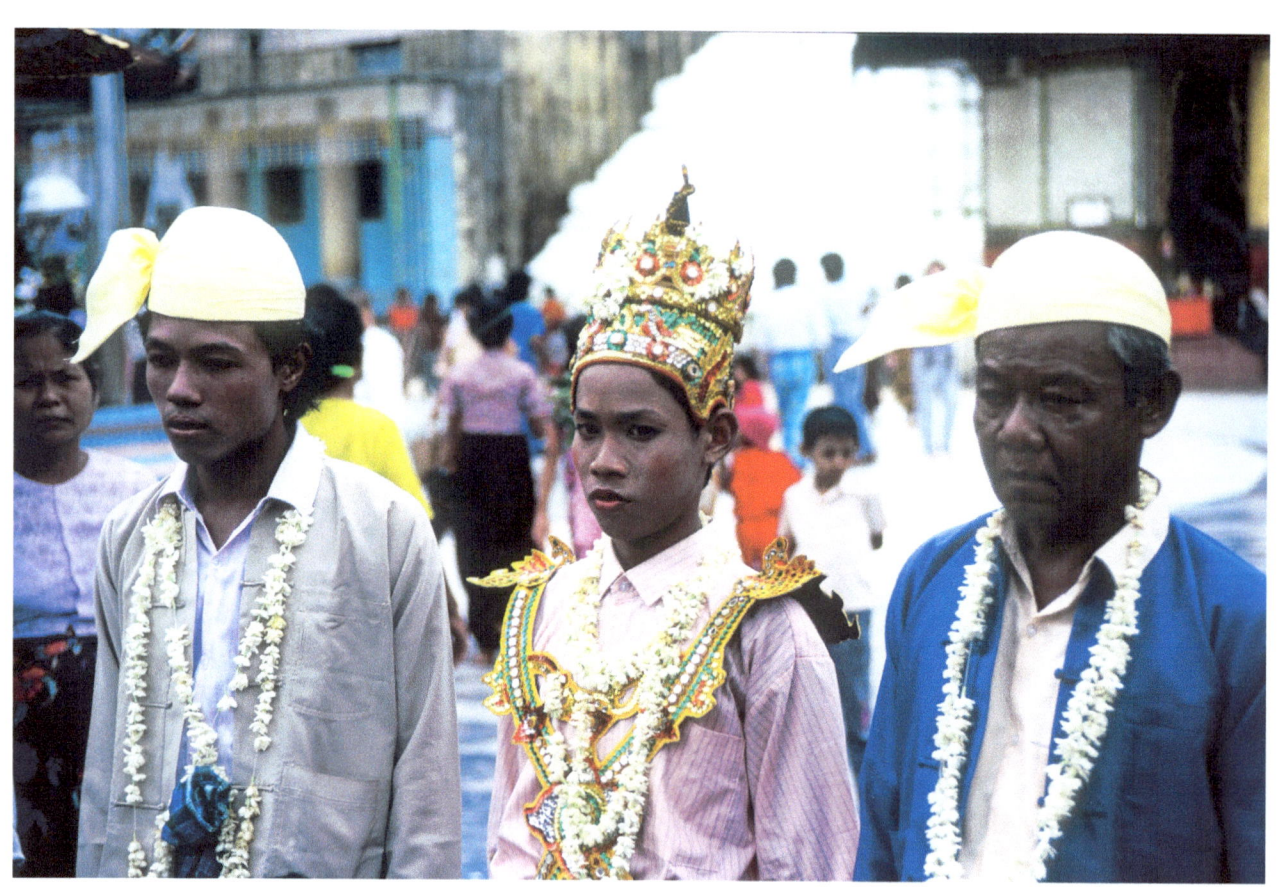

Novitation Ceremony, Shwedagon Pagoda, Yangon, 1988 (above) & 2009

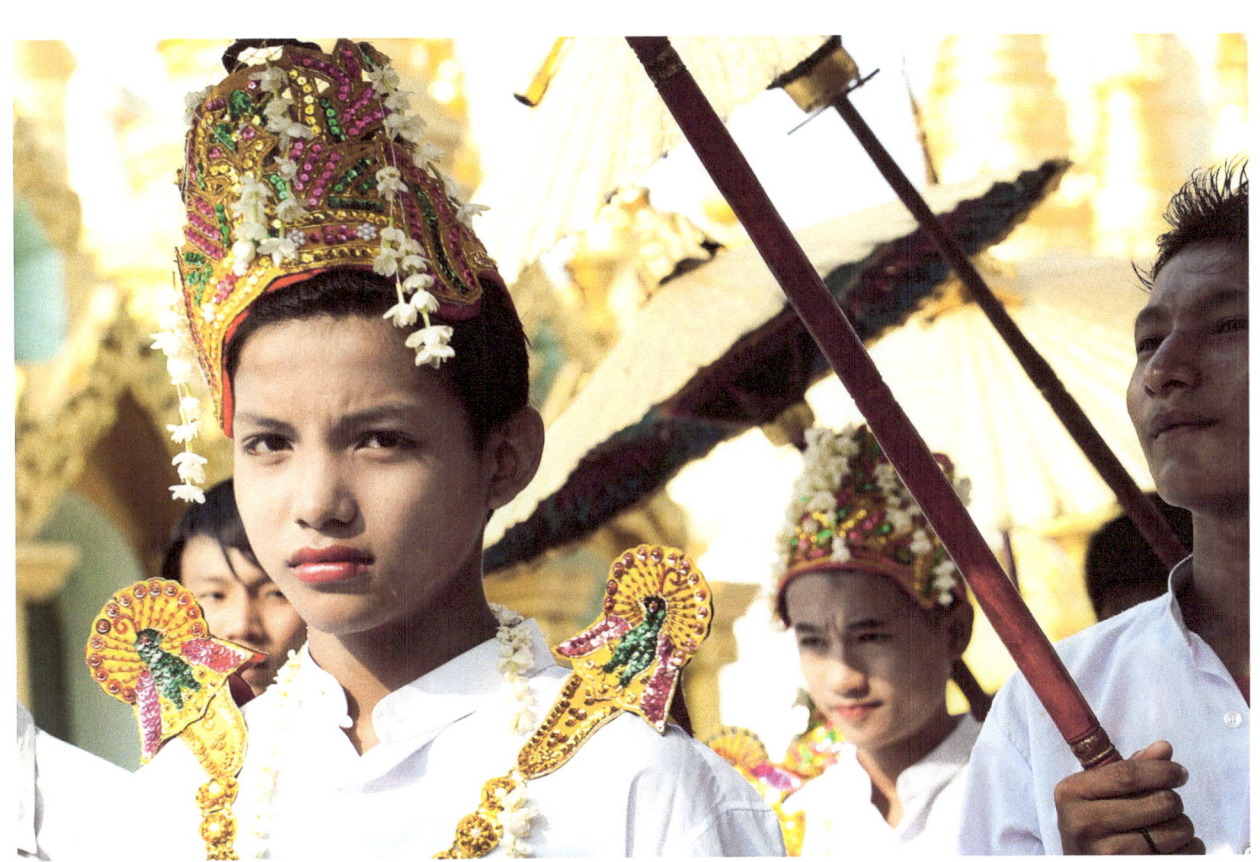

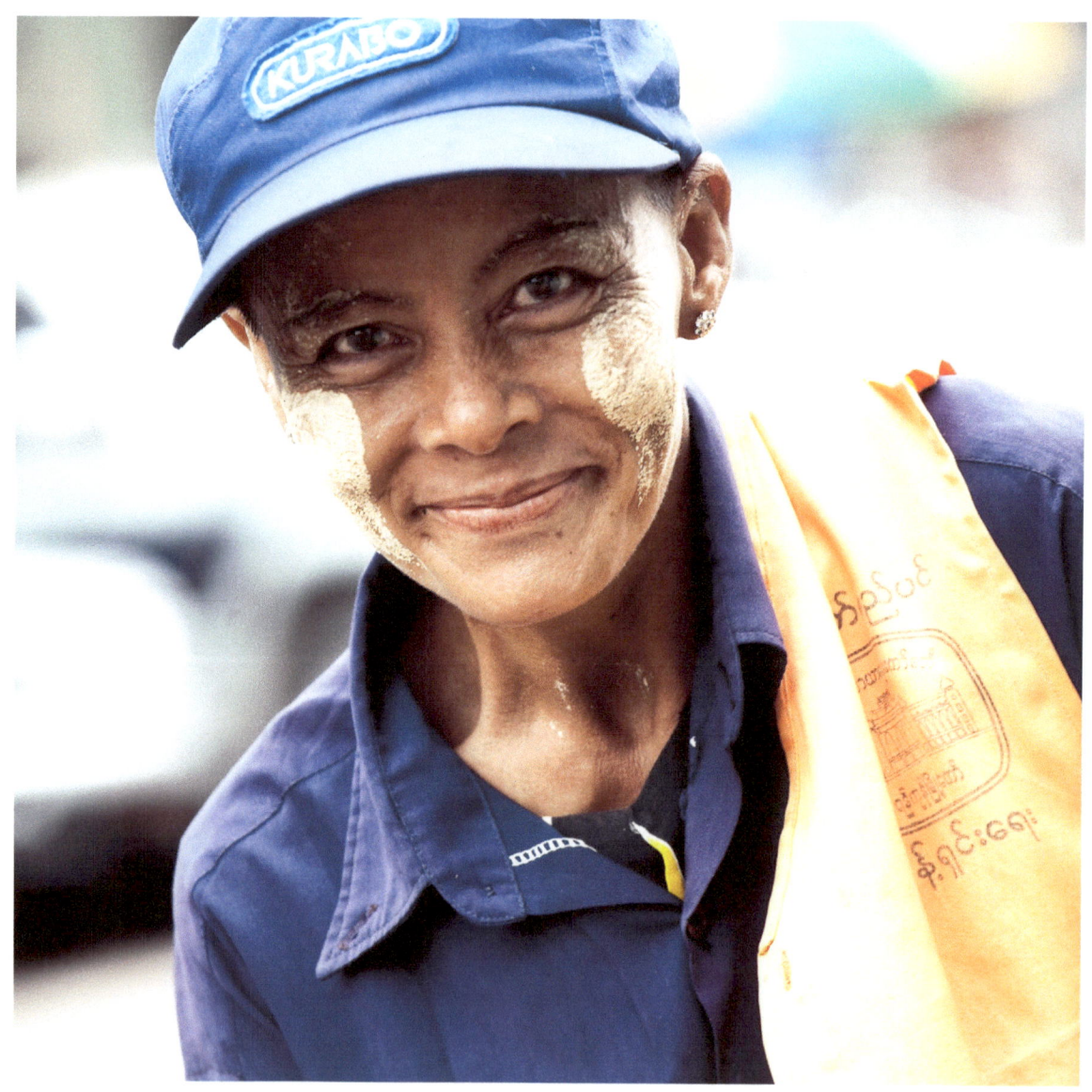

Street Cleaner, Yangon, 2009

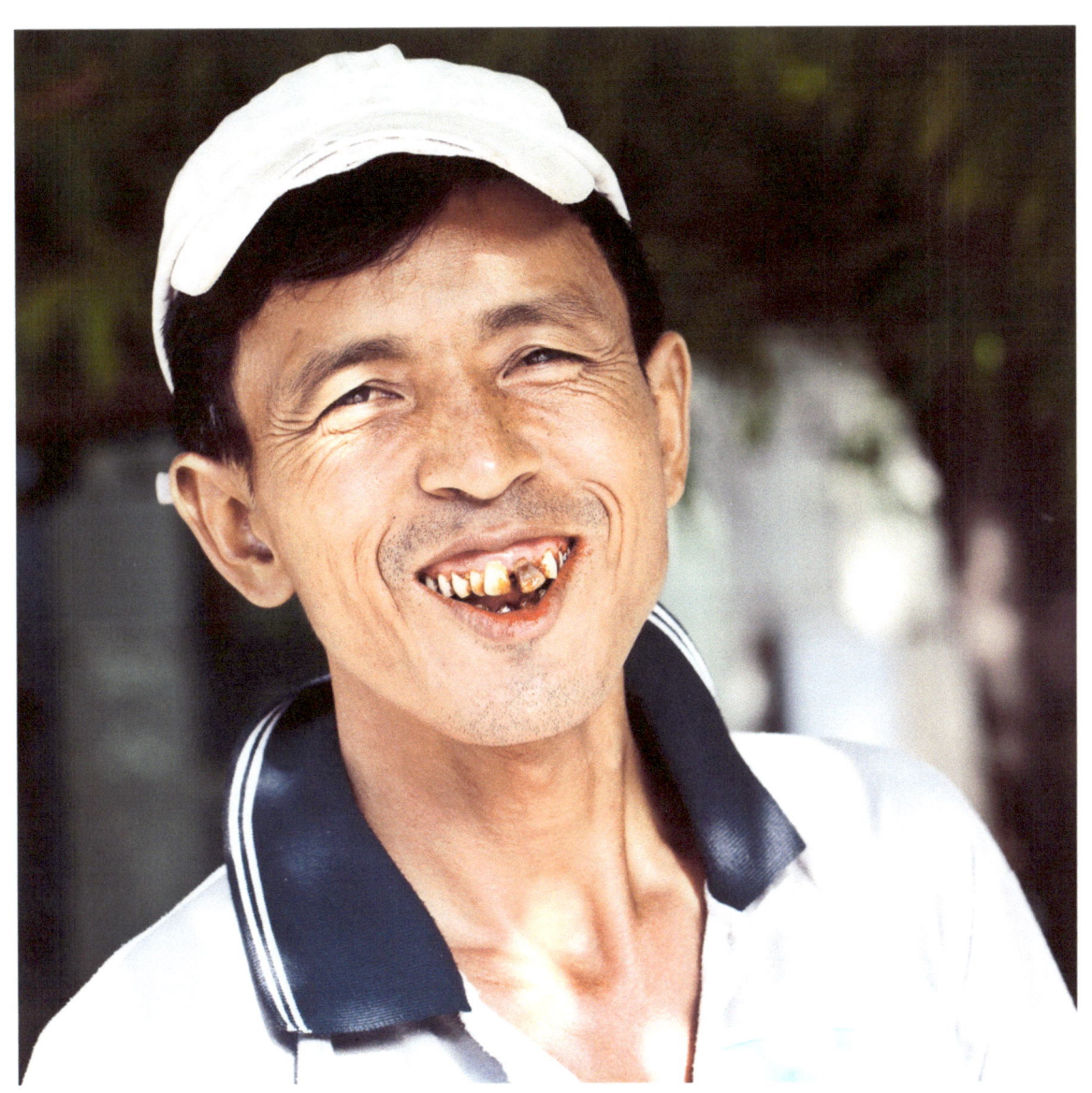

Betel Nut Chewer, Mandalay, 2009

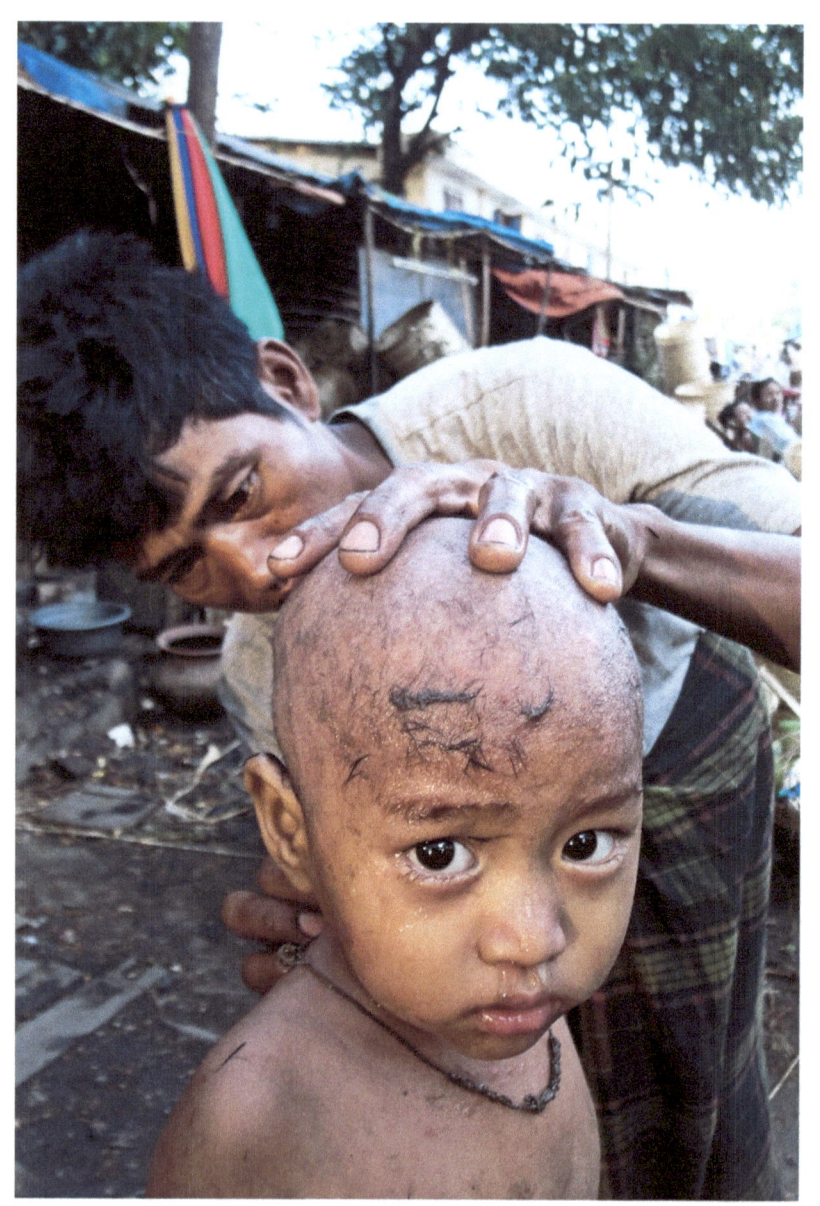

Child having head shaved, Pyay, 2009

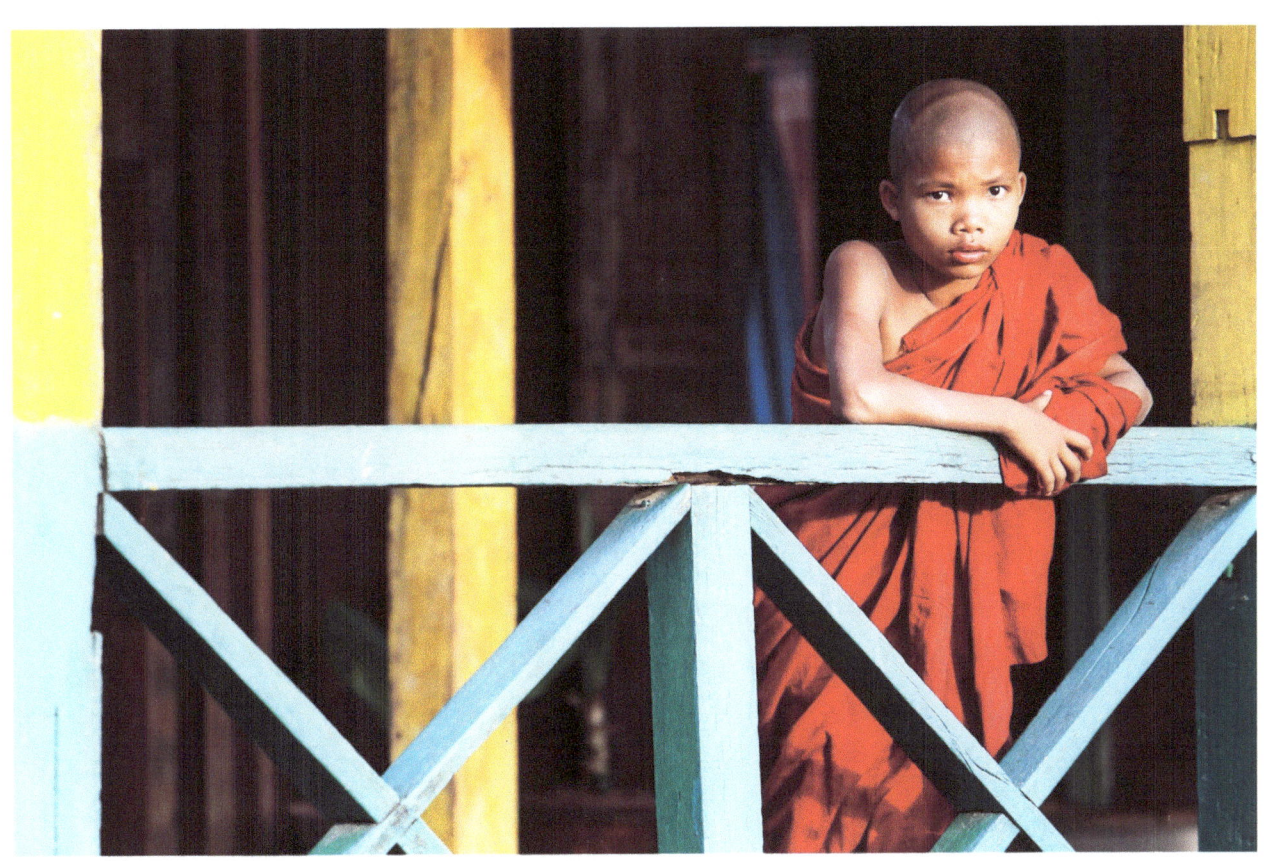

Novice Monk on balcony, Nyaung Shwe, Inle Lake, 2009

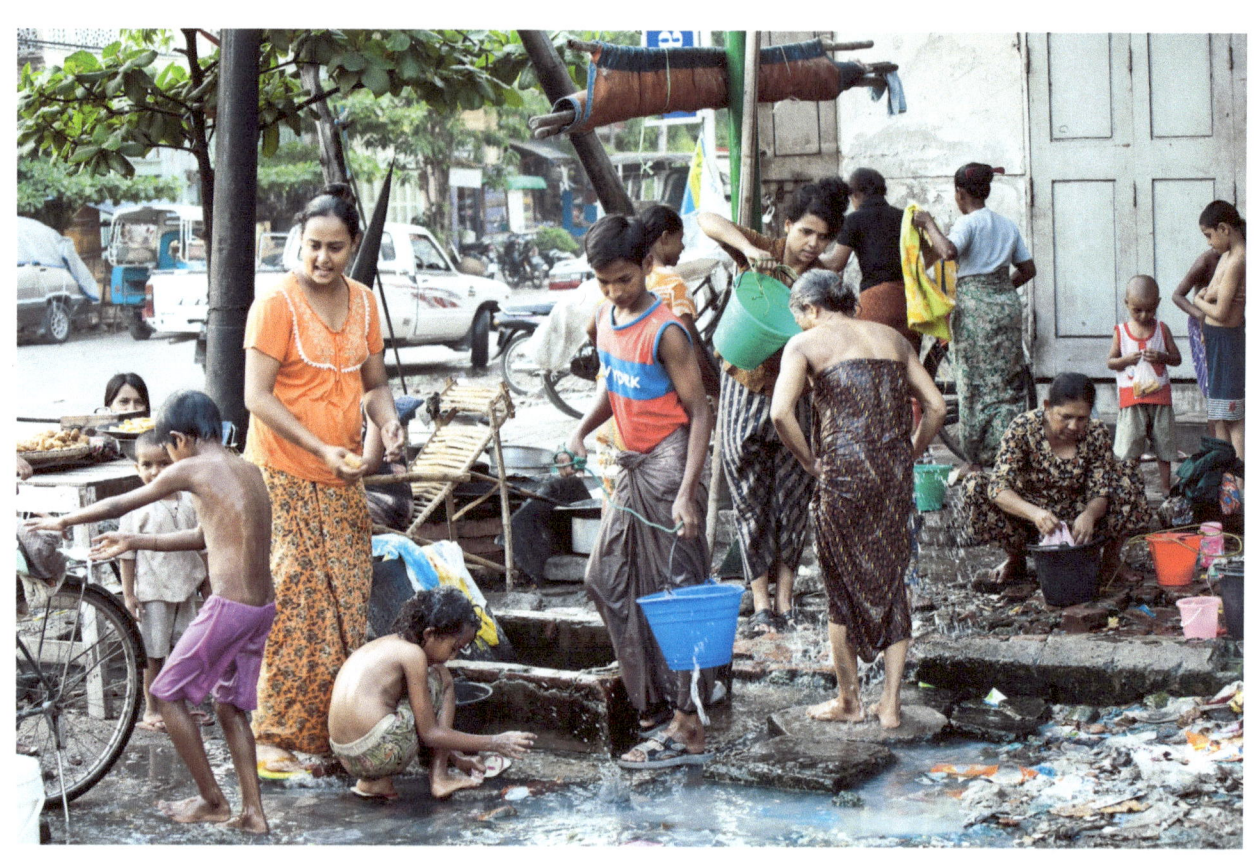

Bathing in street, Mandalay, 2009

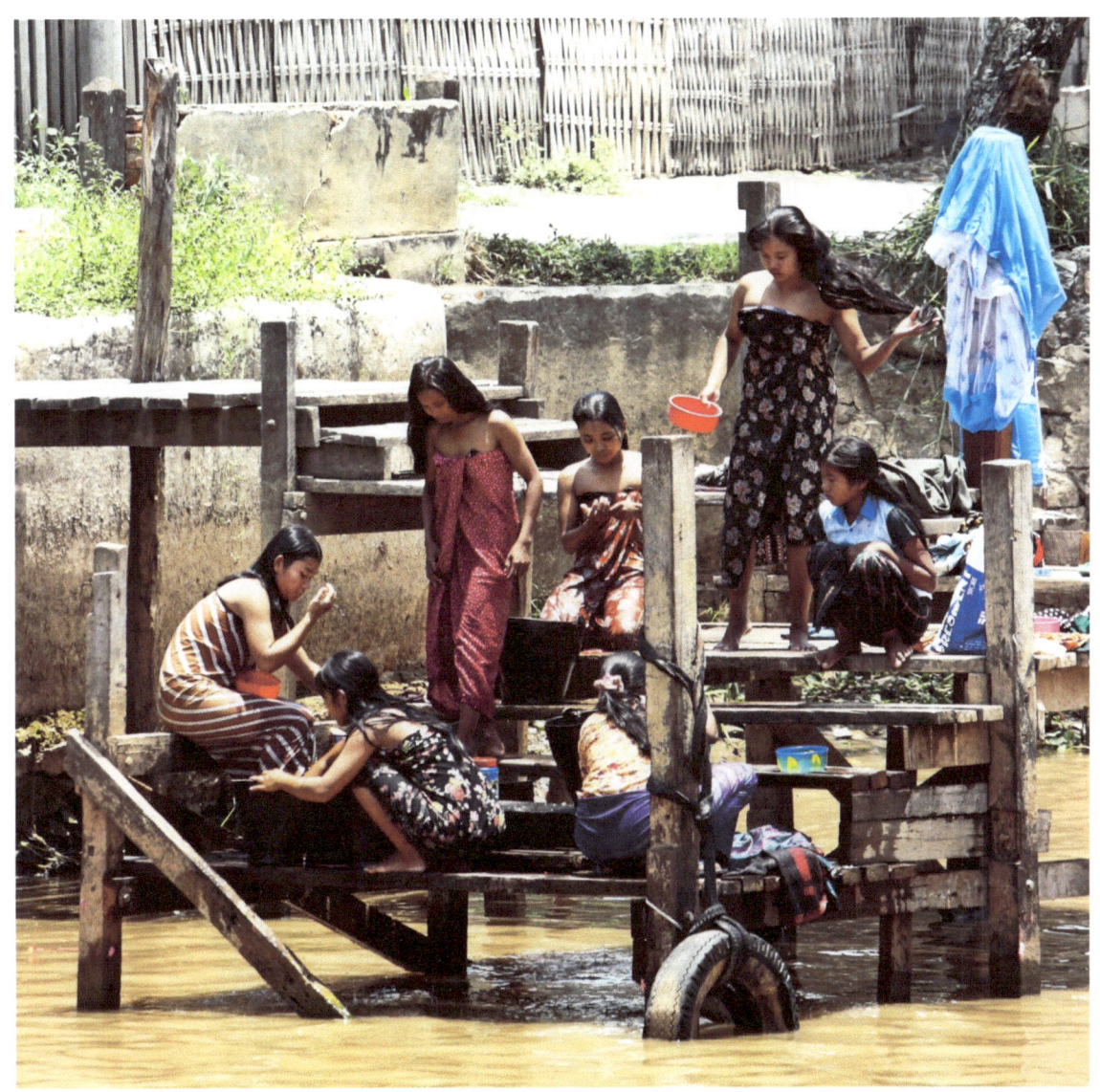

Bath Time, Nyaung Shwe, Inle Lake, 2009

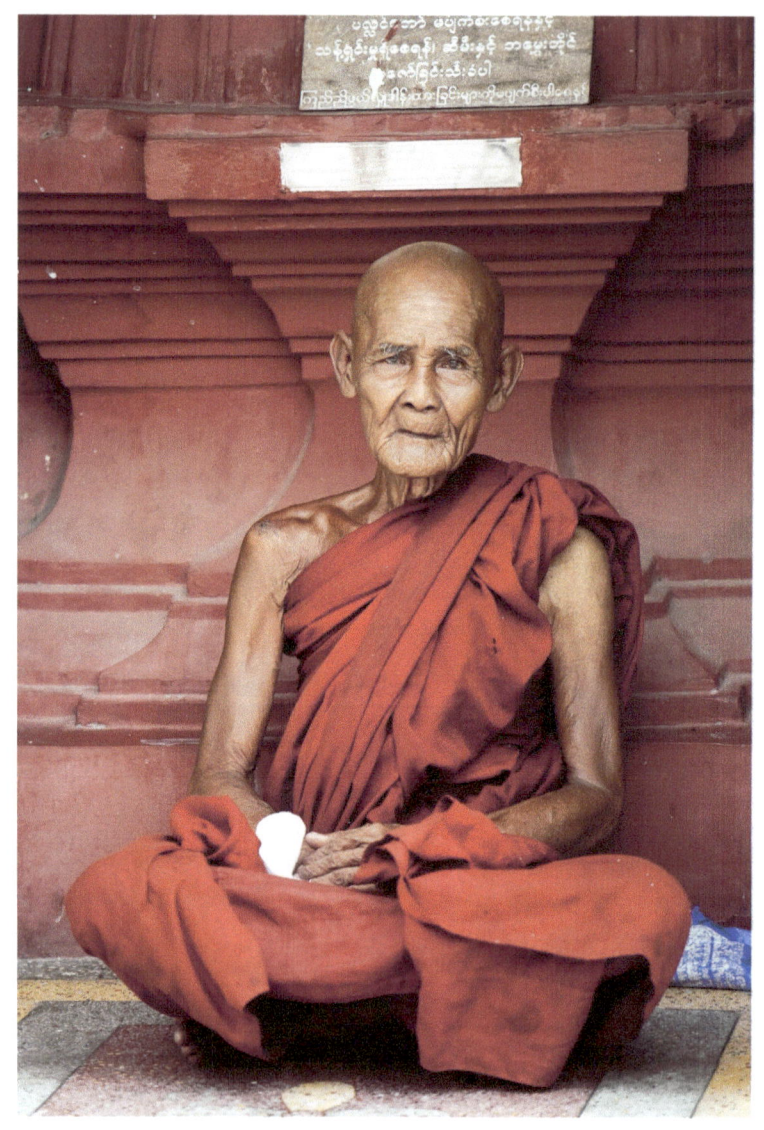

Elderly Monk, Shwedagon Pagoda, Yangon, 2009

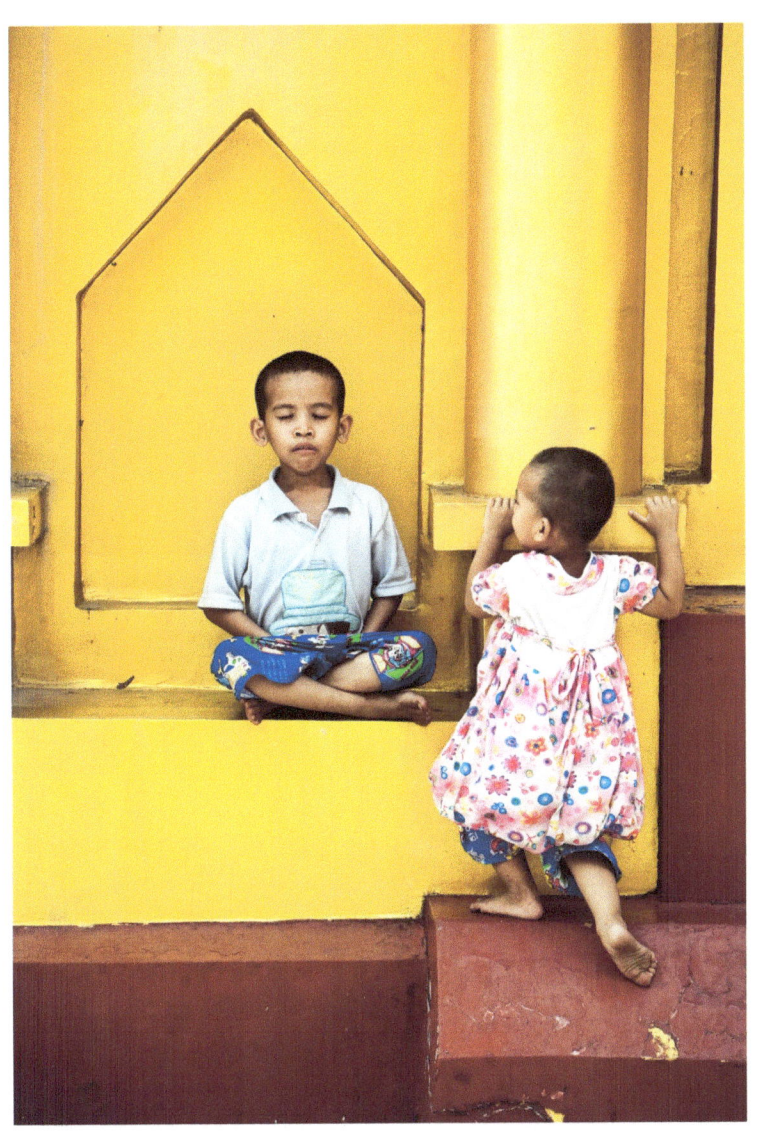

Pretending to pray, Shwedagon Pagoda, Yangon, 2009

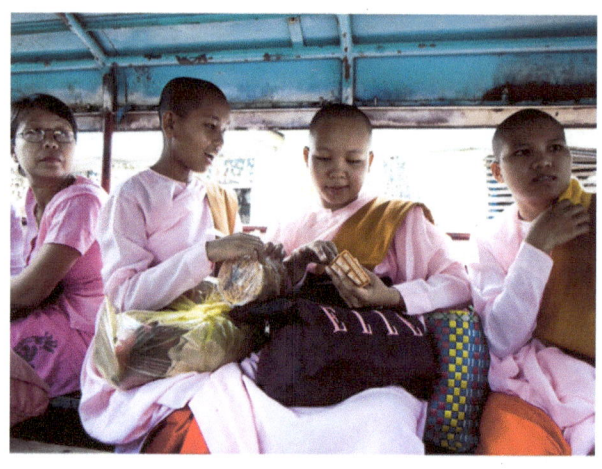
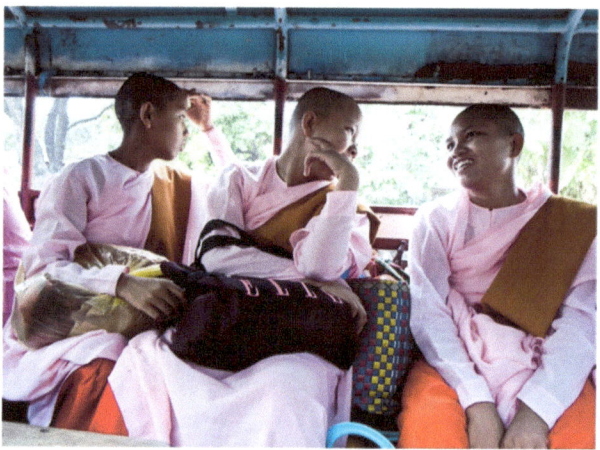
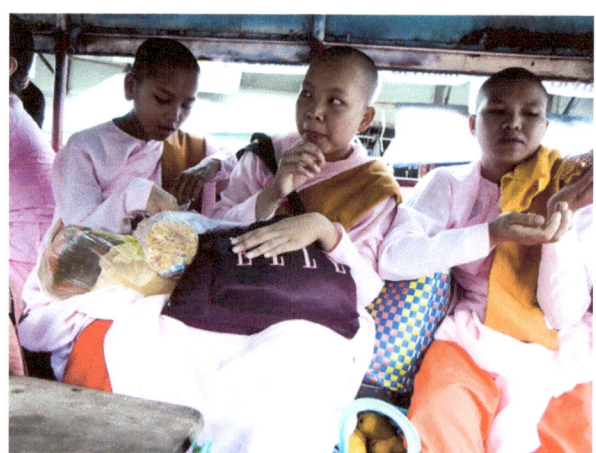
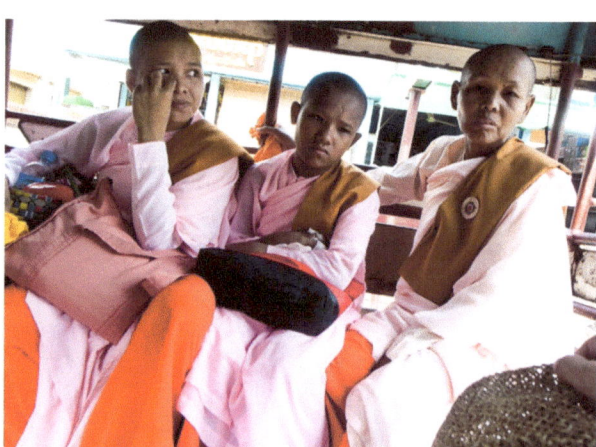

Nuns on bus, Mandalay, 2009

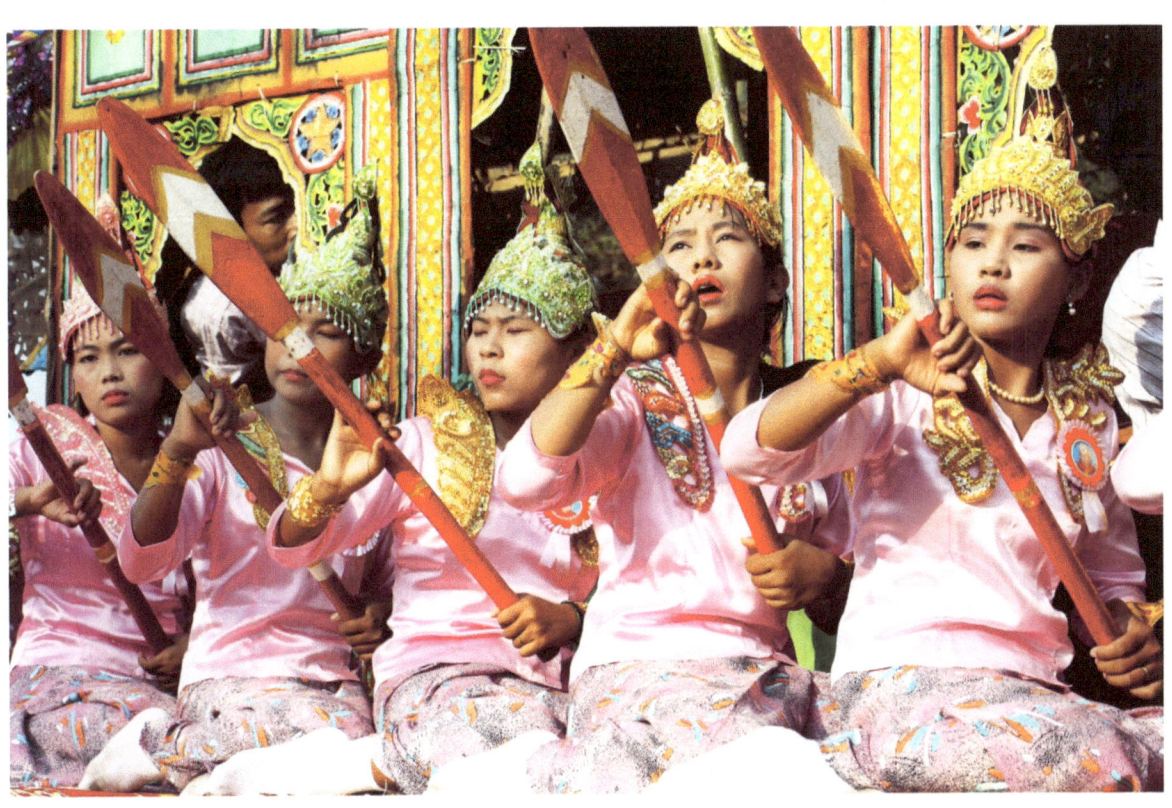

Performers at funeral procession, Bagan, 2009

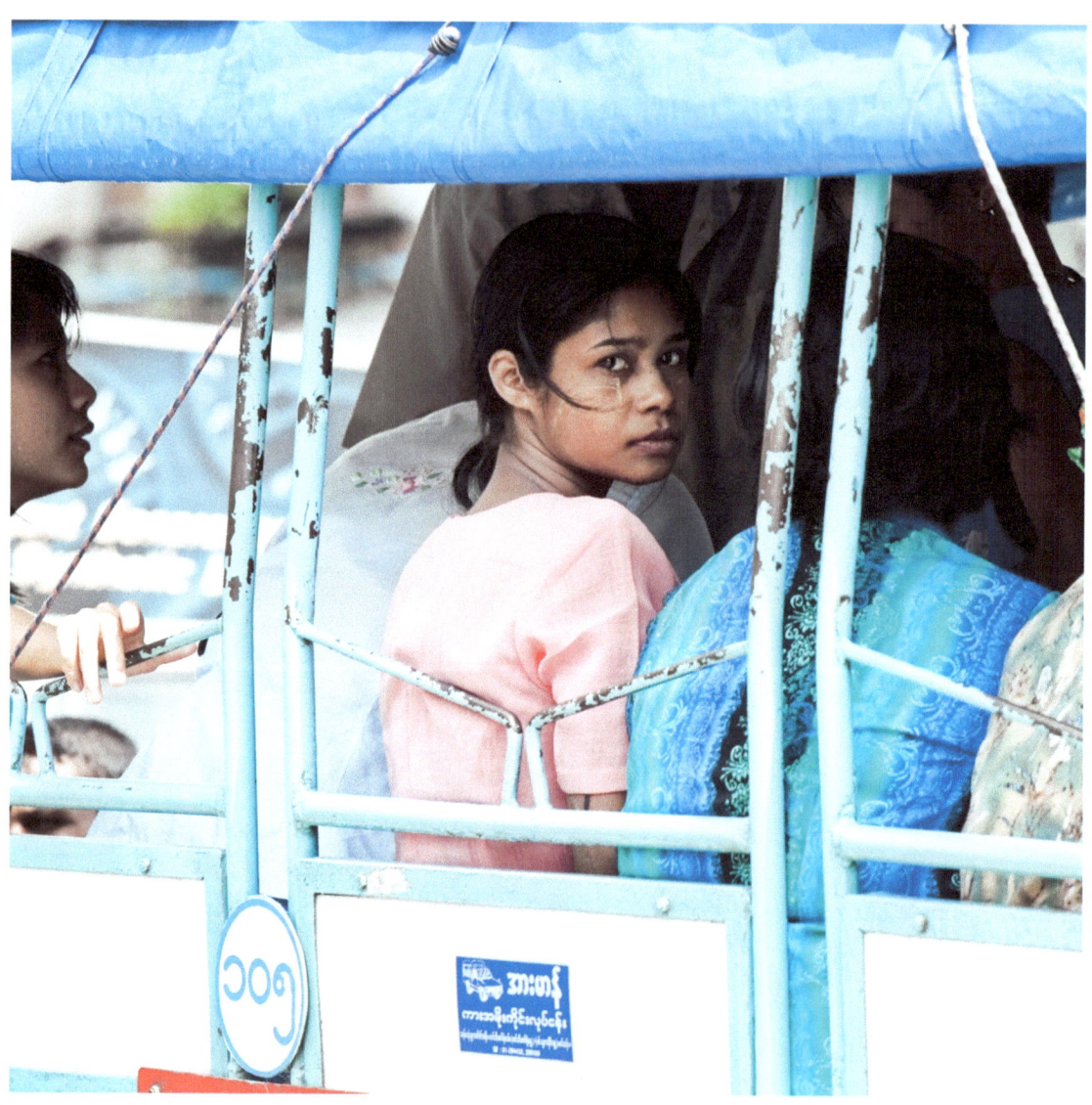

Young female on bus, Yangon, 2009

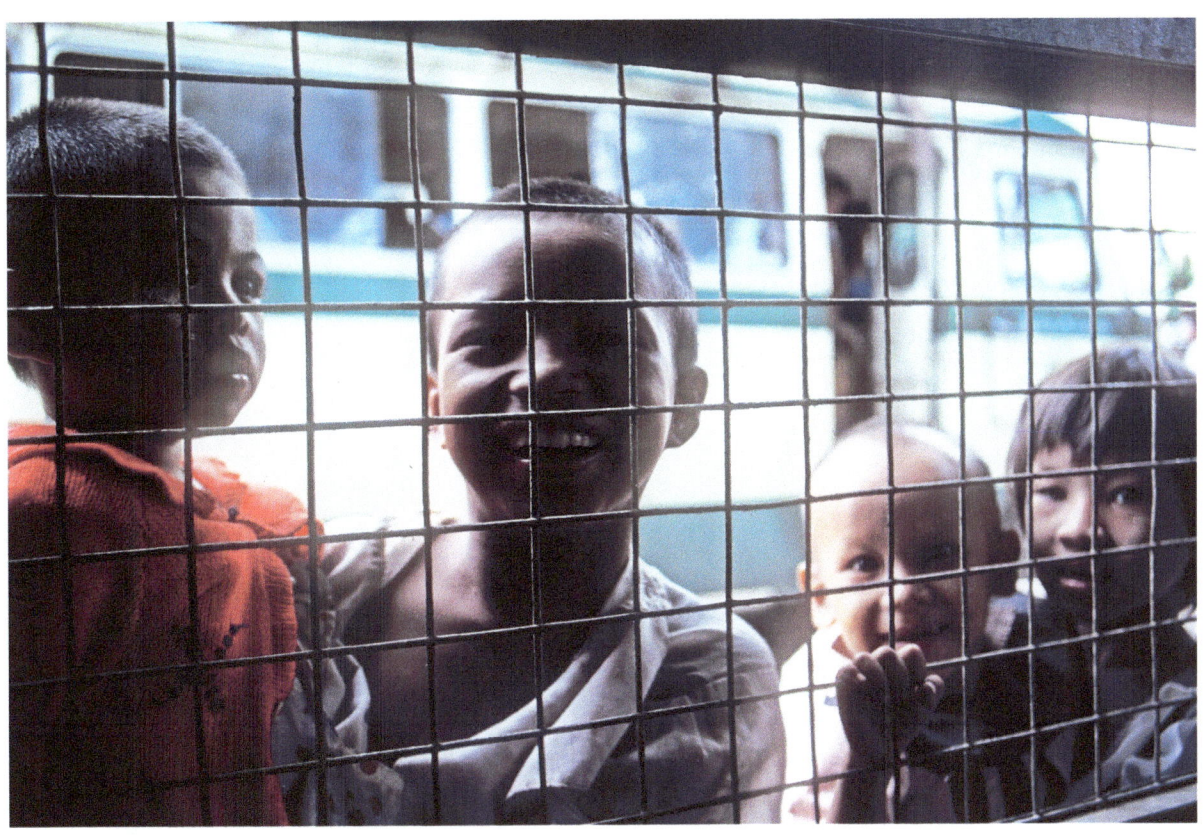

Restaurant stop on the way to Mandalay, 1988

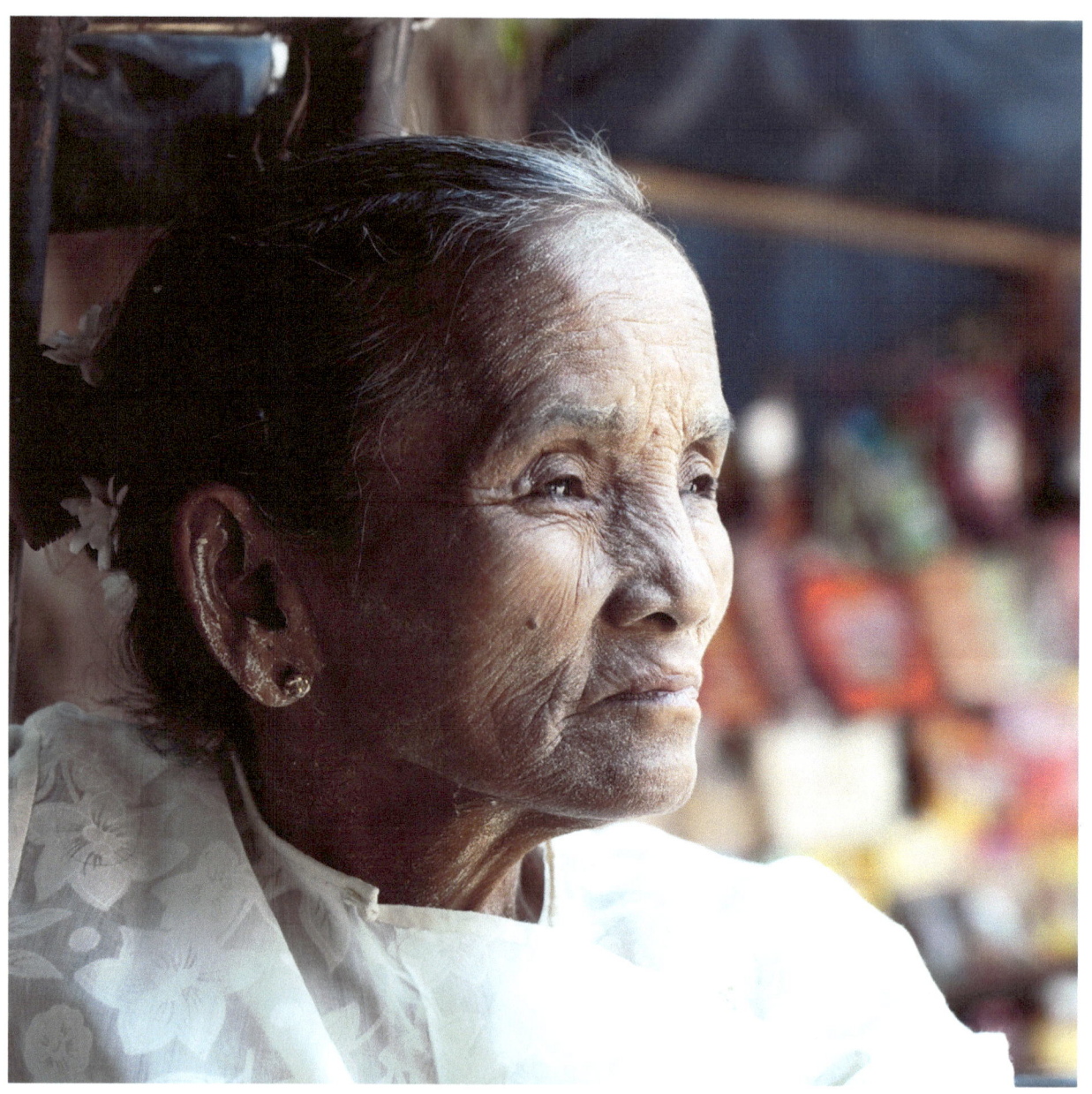

Elderly woman on bus on the way to Bagan, 2009

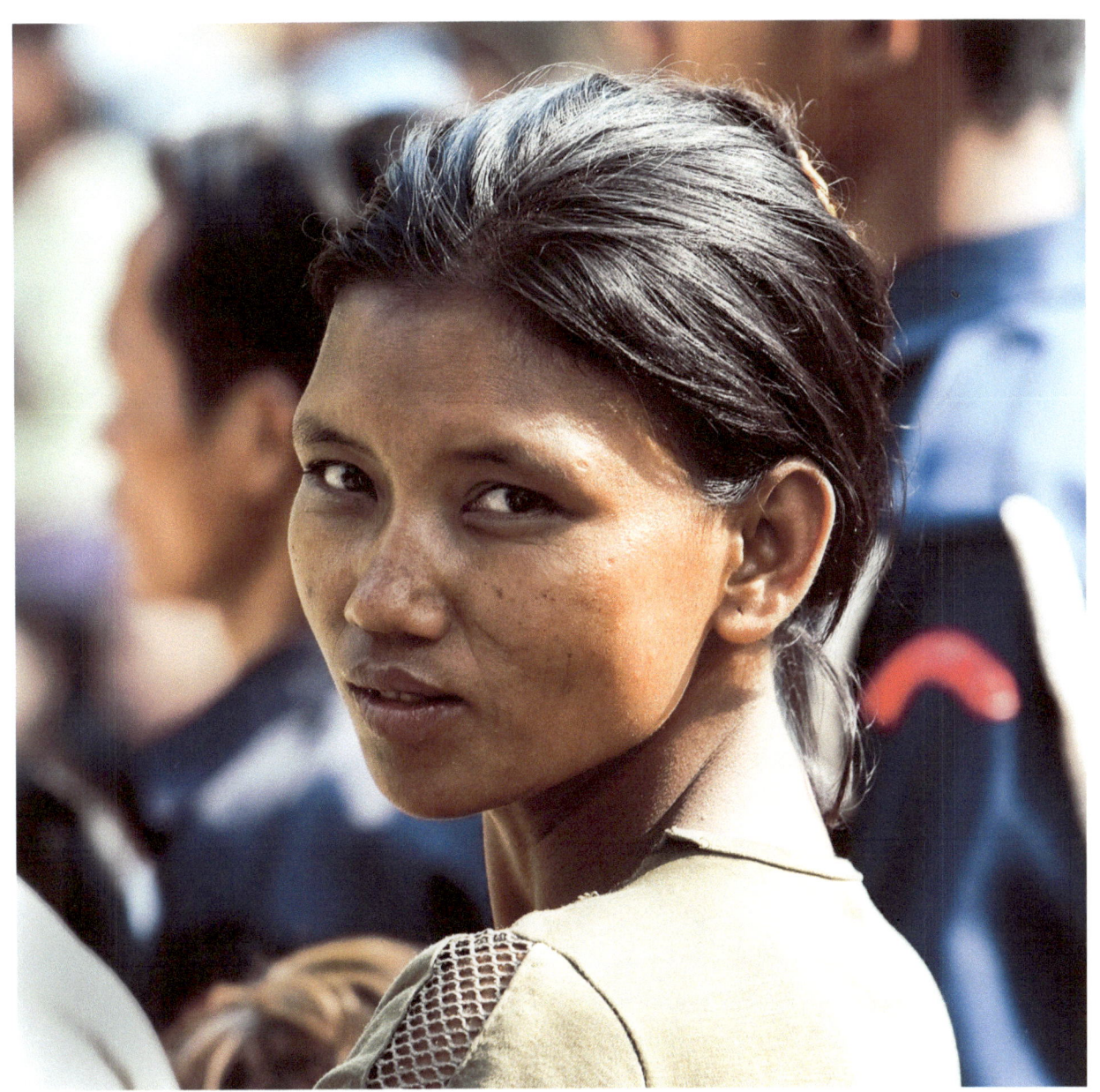

Woman in crowd at funeral procession, Bagan, 2009

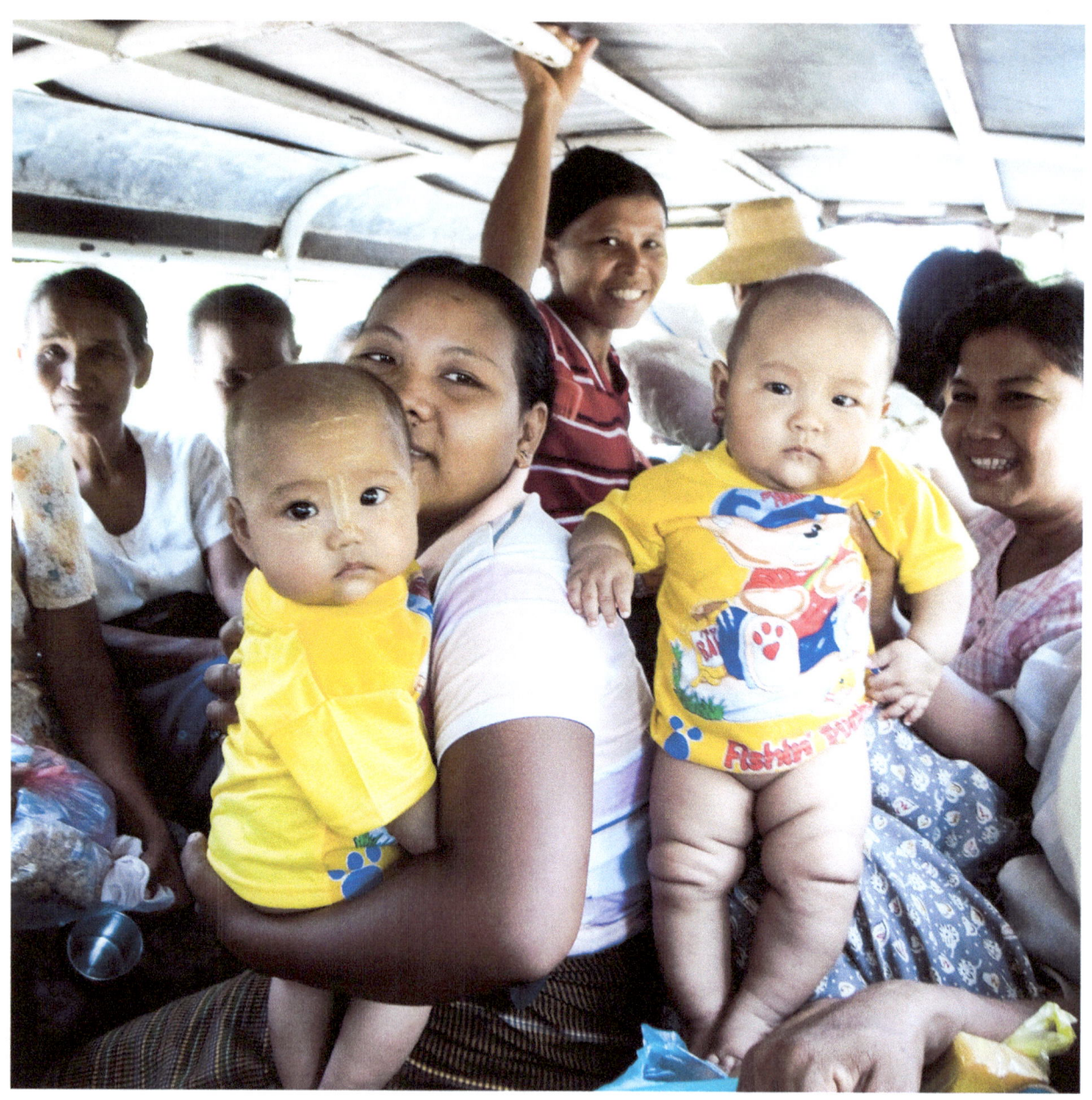

Locals on bus, Monywa, 2009

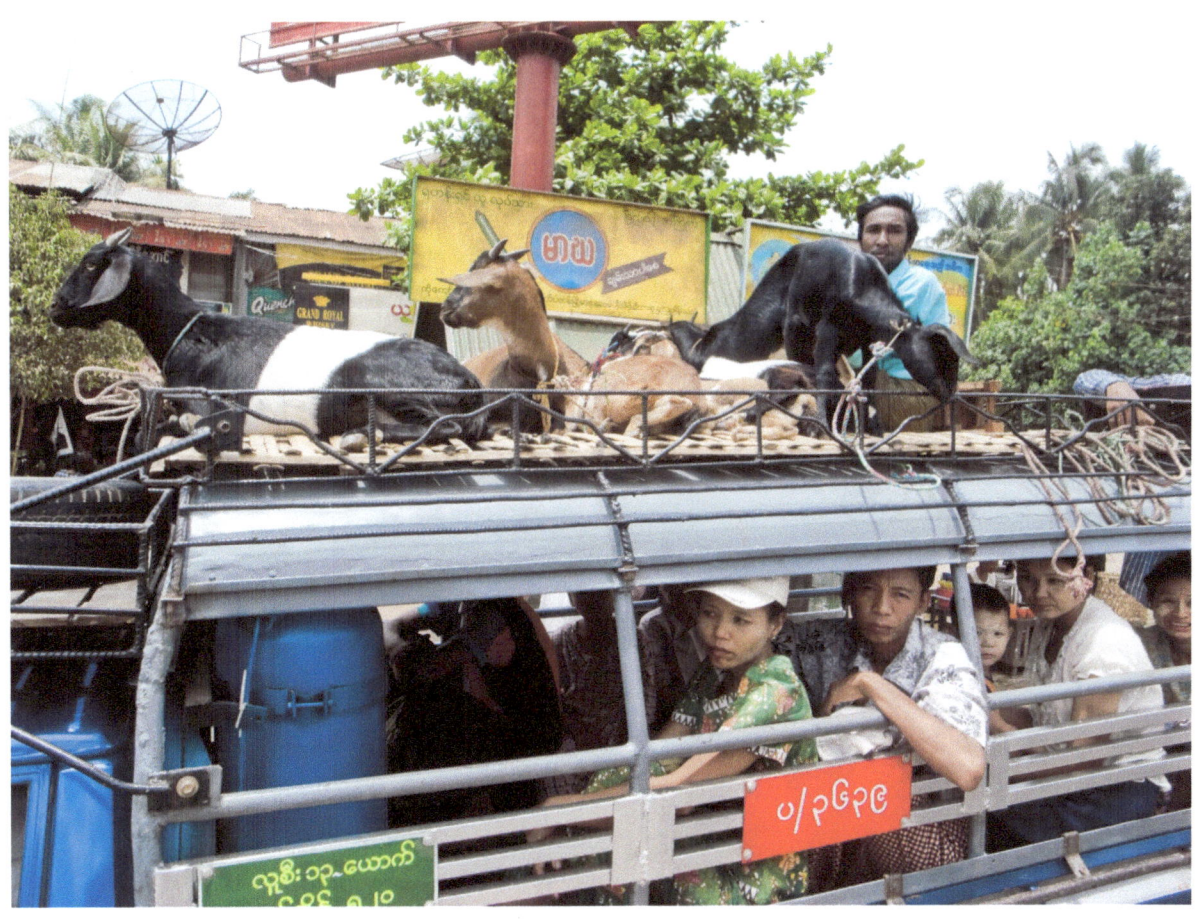

Locals on bus on the way to Pyay, 2009

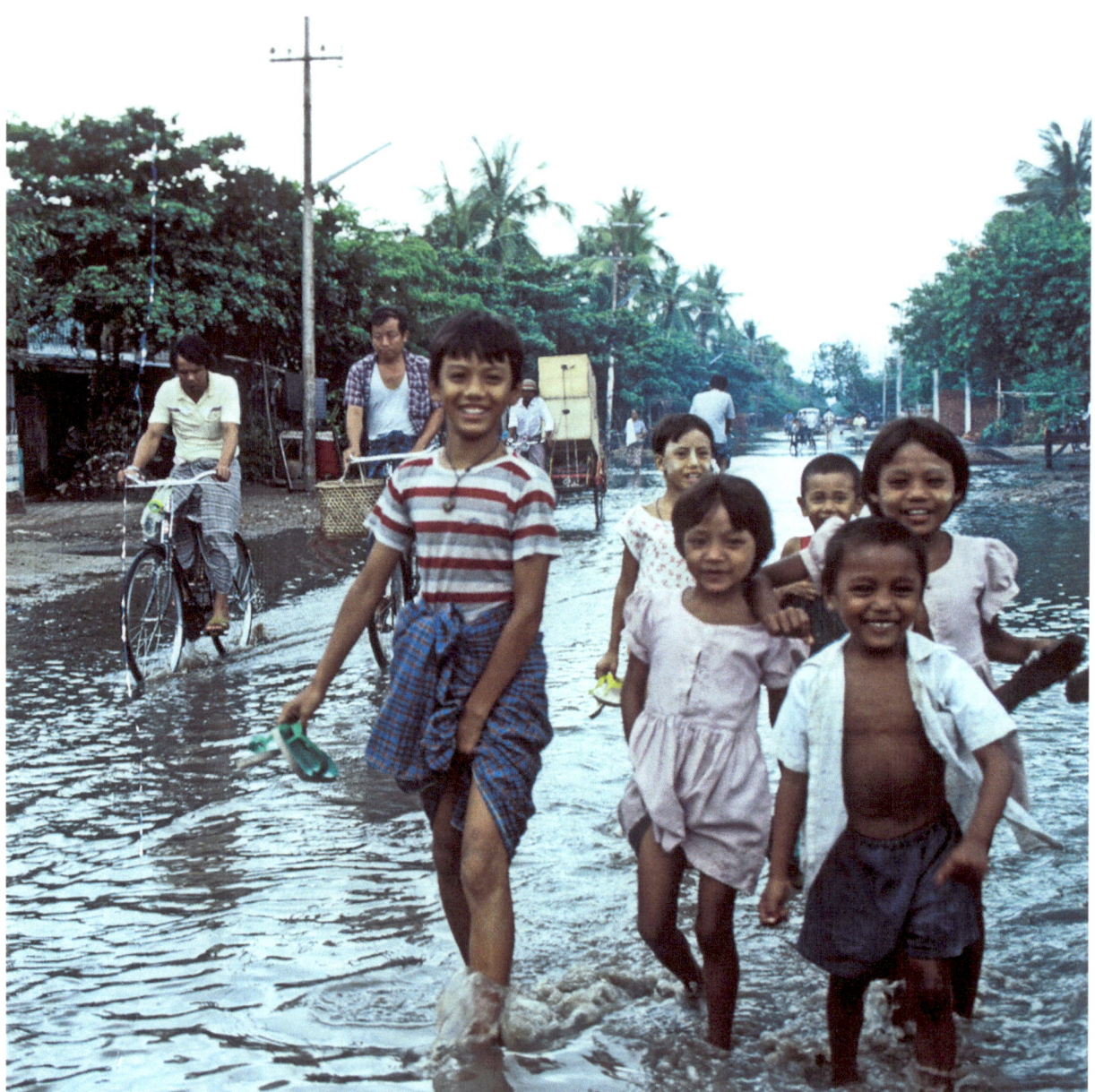

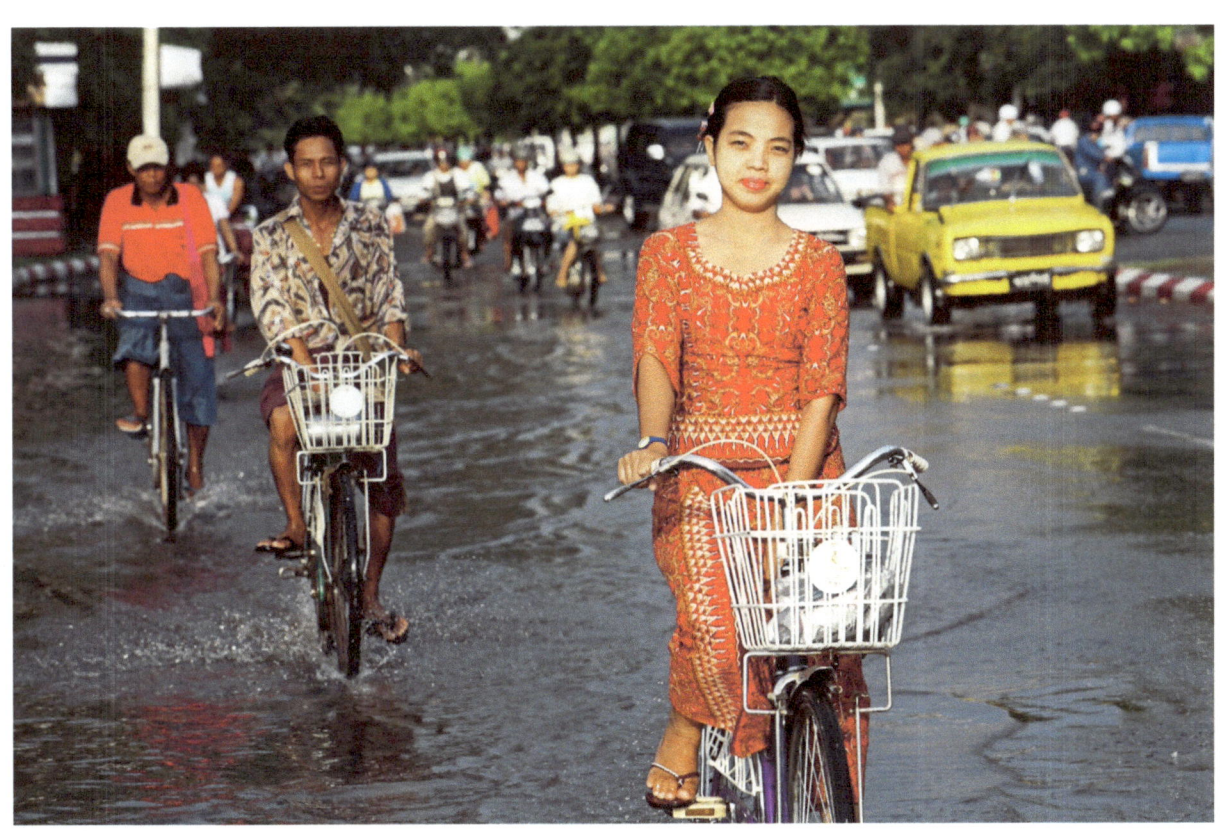

After the showers in Mandalay, 1988 (opposite), 2009 (above)

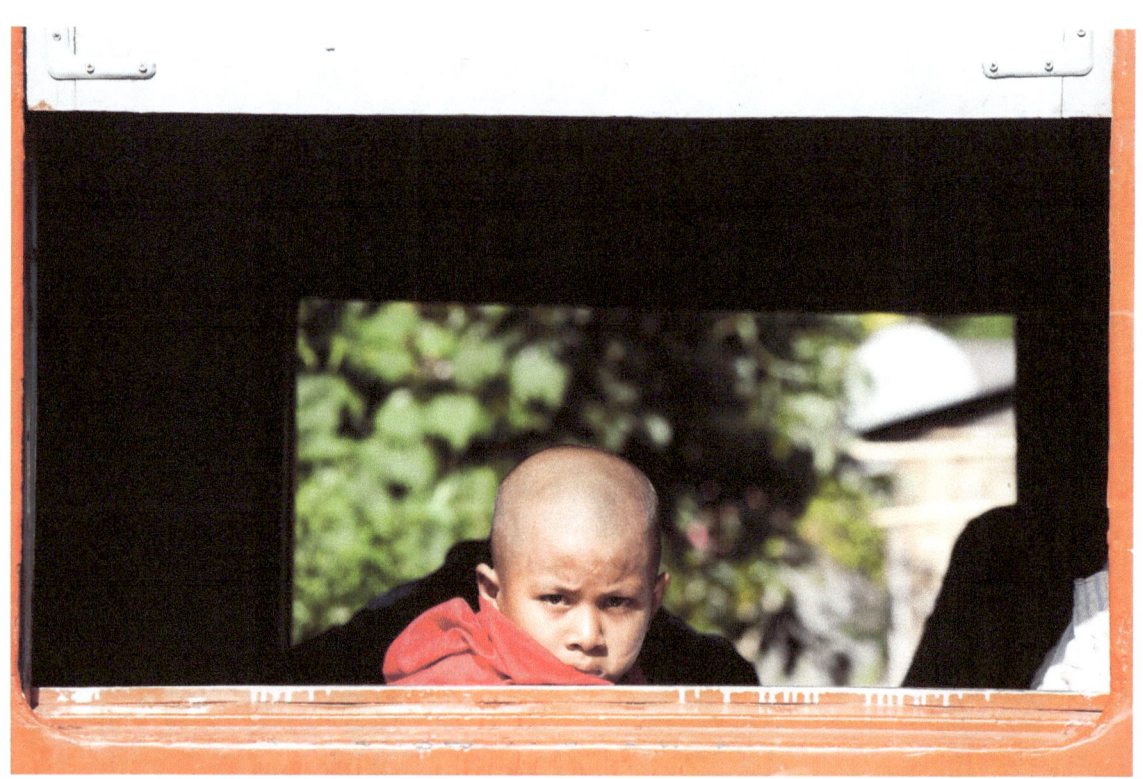

Novice Monk waiting for train to depart, Kalaw, 2009

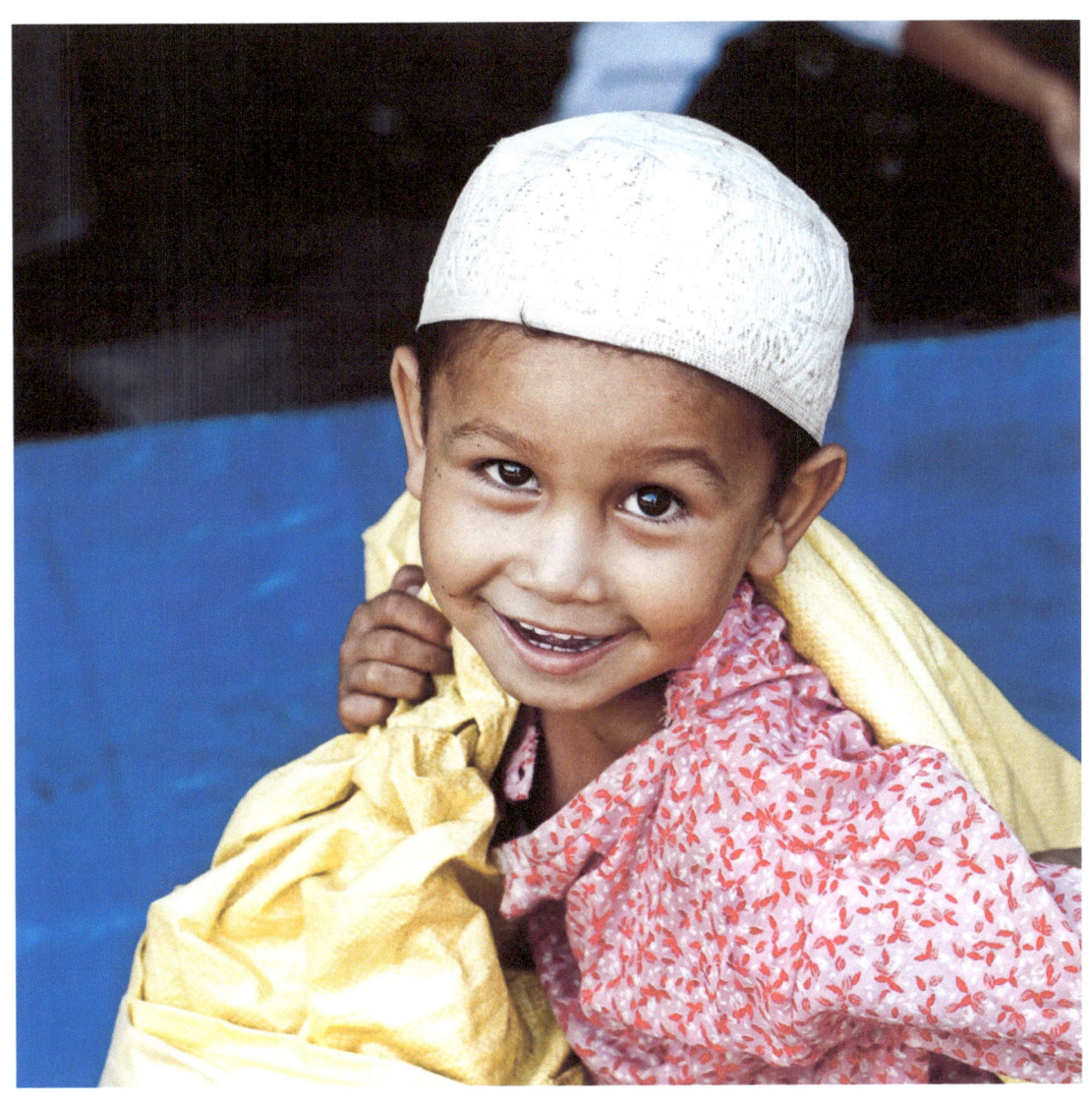

Young Muslim at Market, Maing Thauk, Inle Lake, 2009

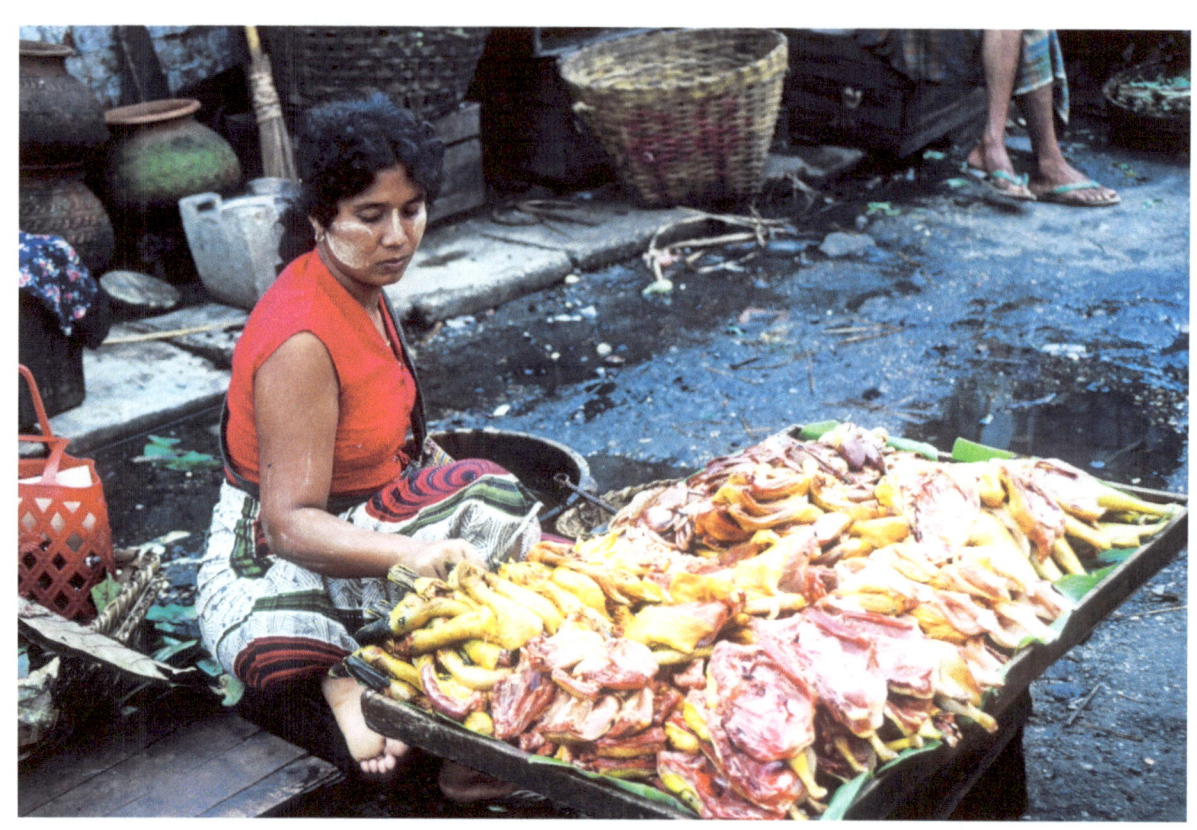

Market Trader, Yangon, 1988

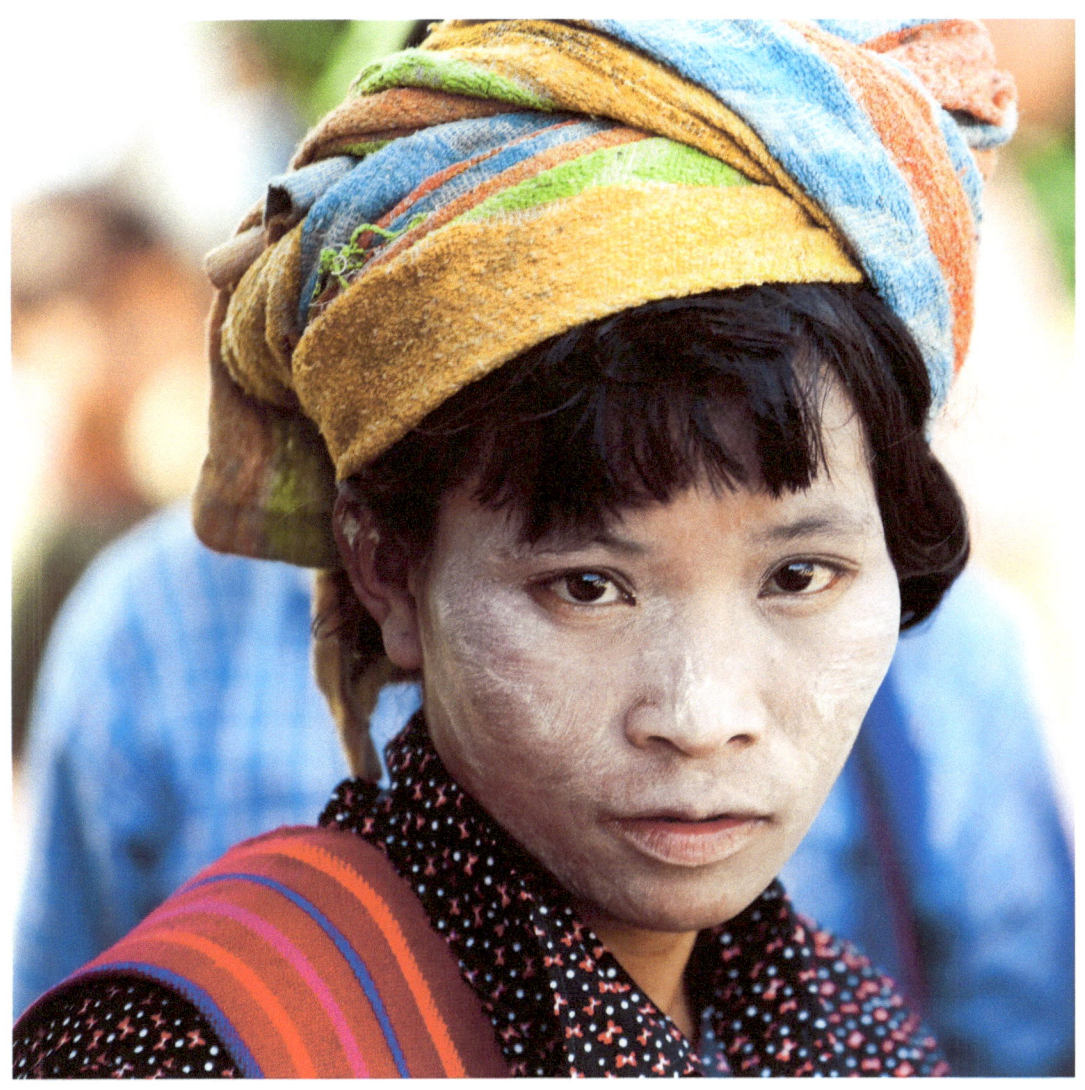

Woman at Market, Maing Thauk, Inle Lake, 2009

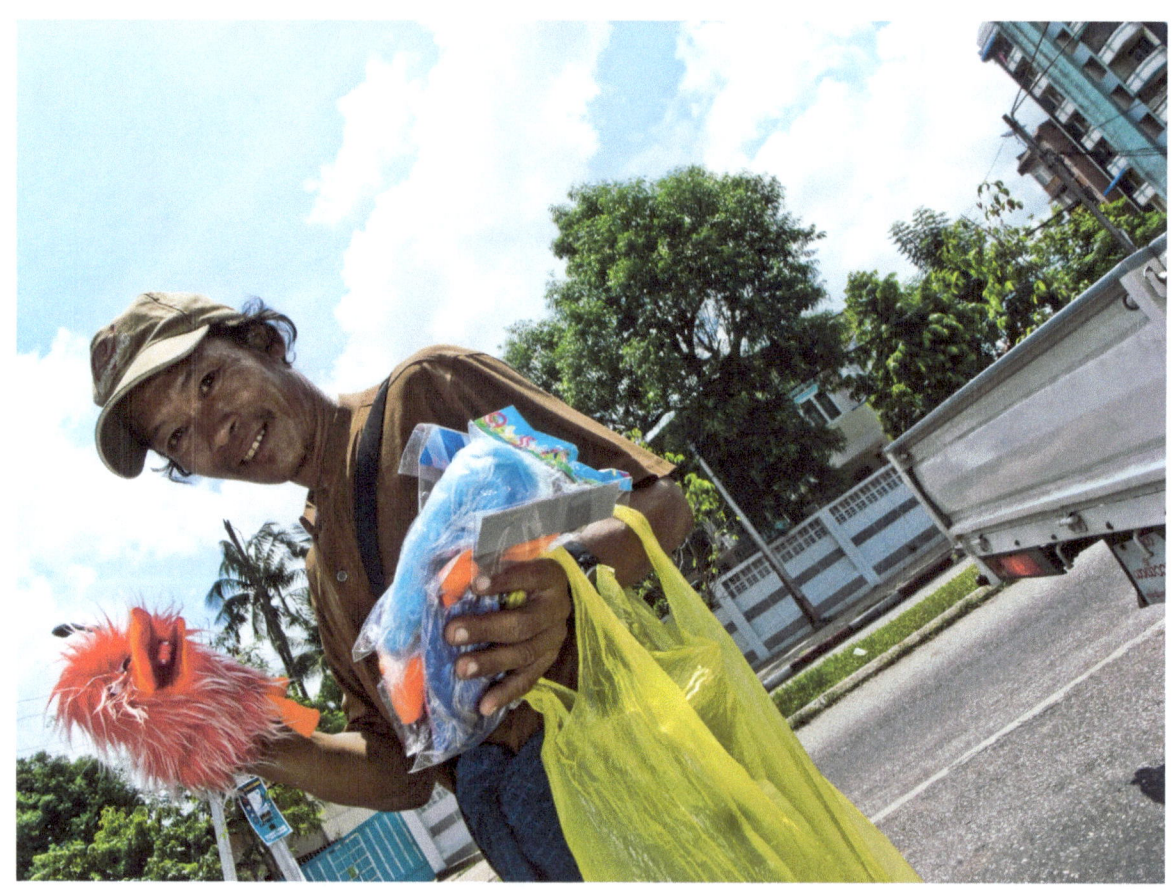

Puppet Salesman at car window, Yangon, 2009

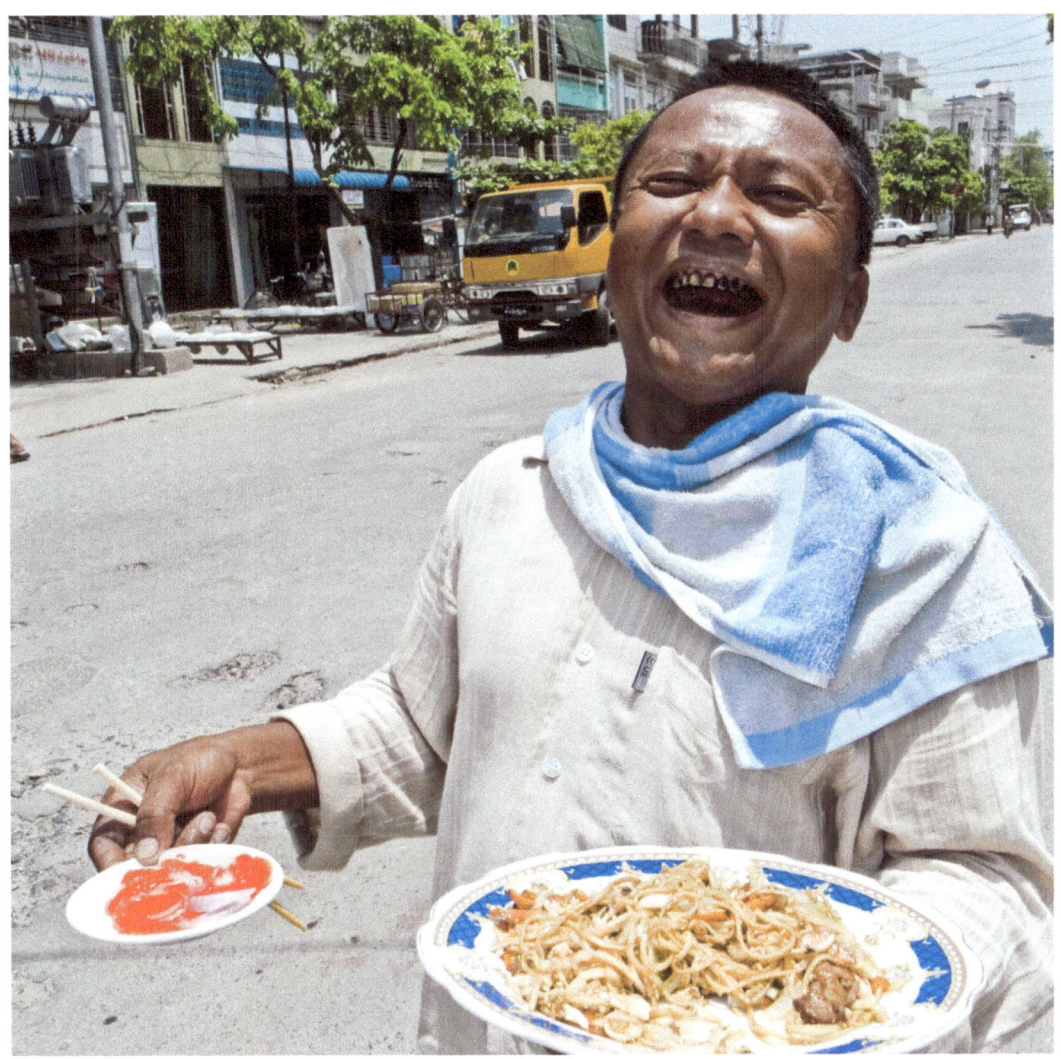

Money Changer, Mandalay, 2009

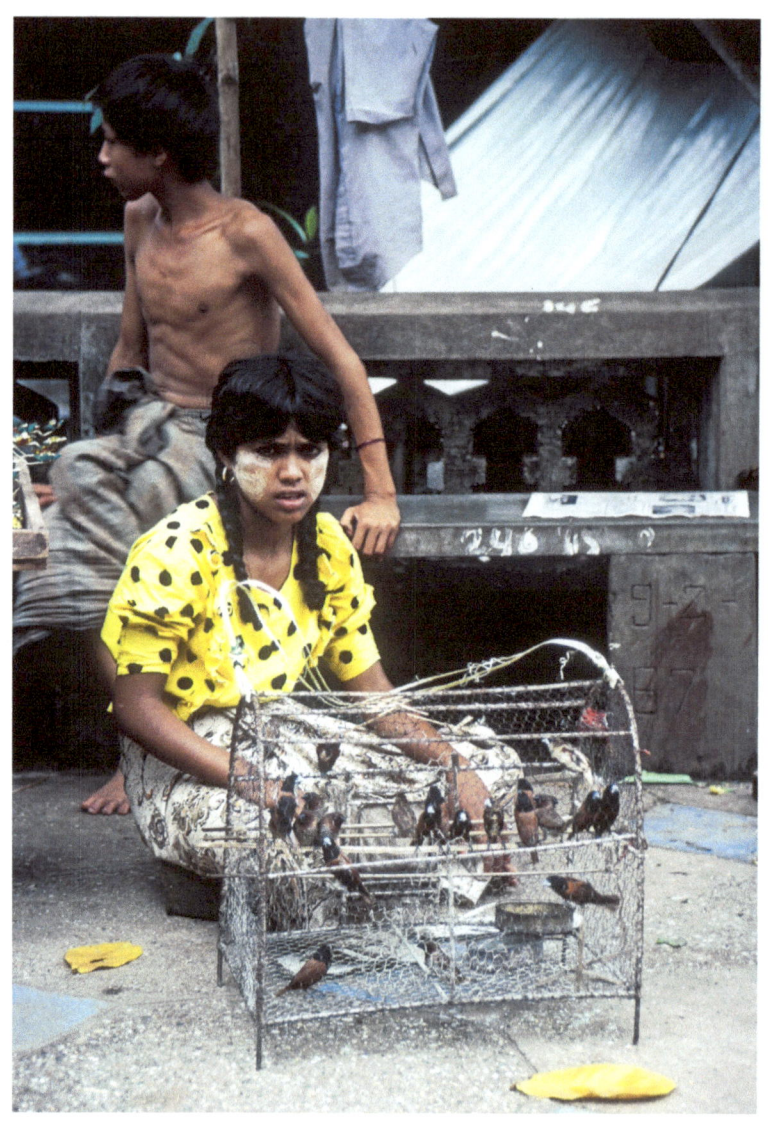

Selling birds for release, Shwedagon Pagoda, Yangon, 1988

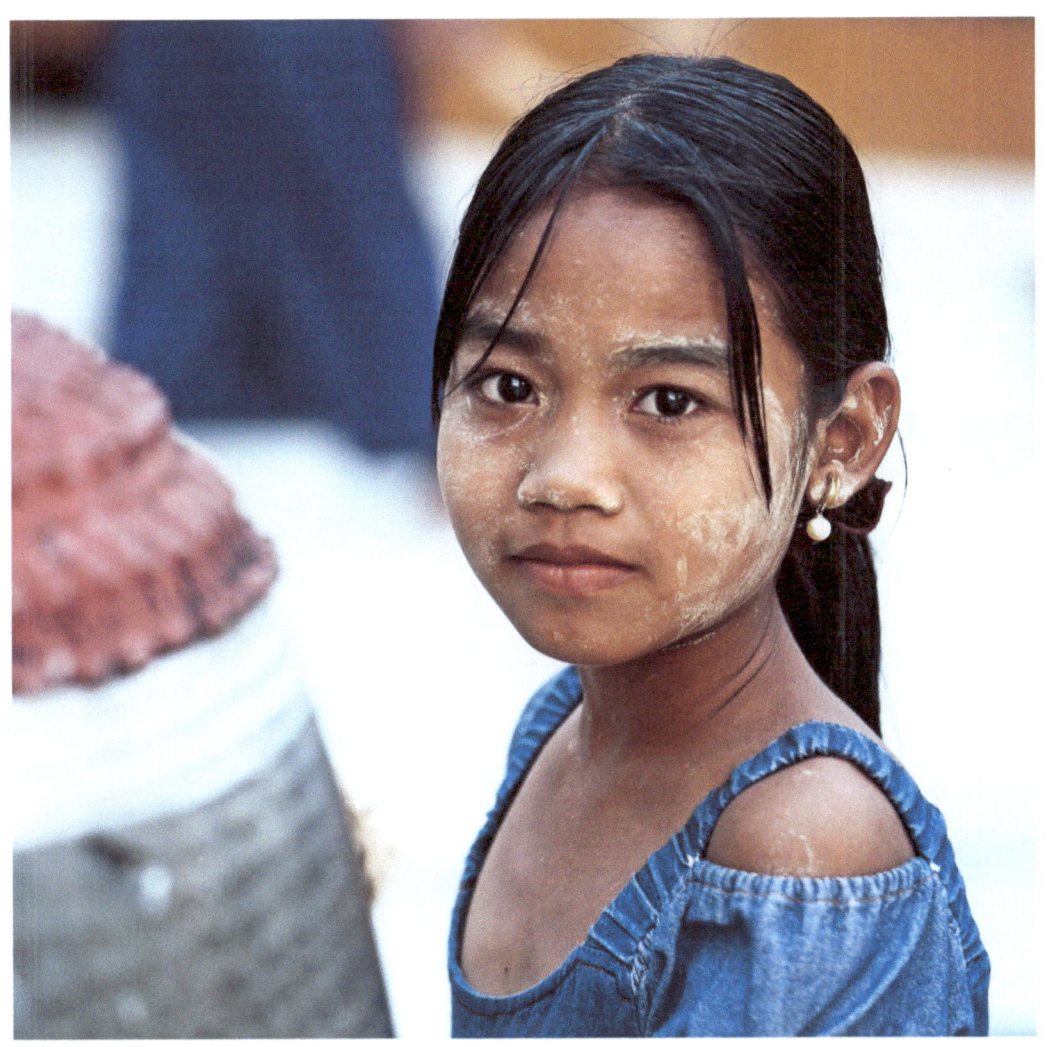

Young girl at Shwedagon Pagoda, Yangon, 2009

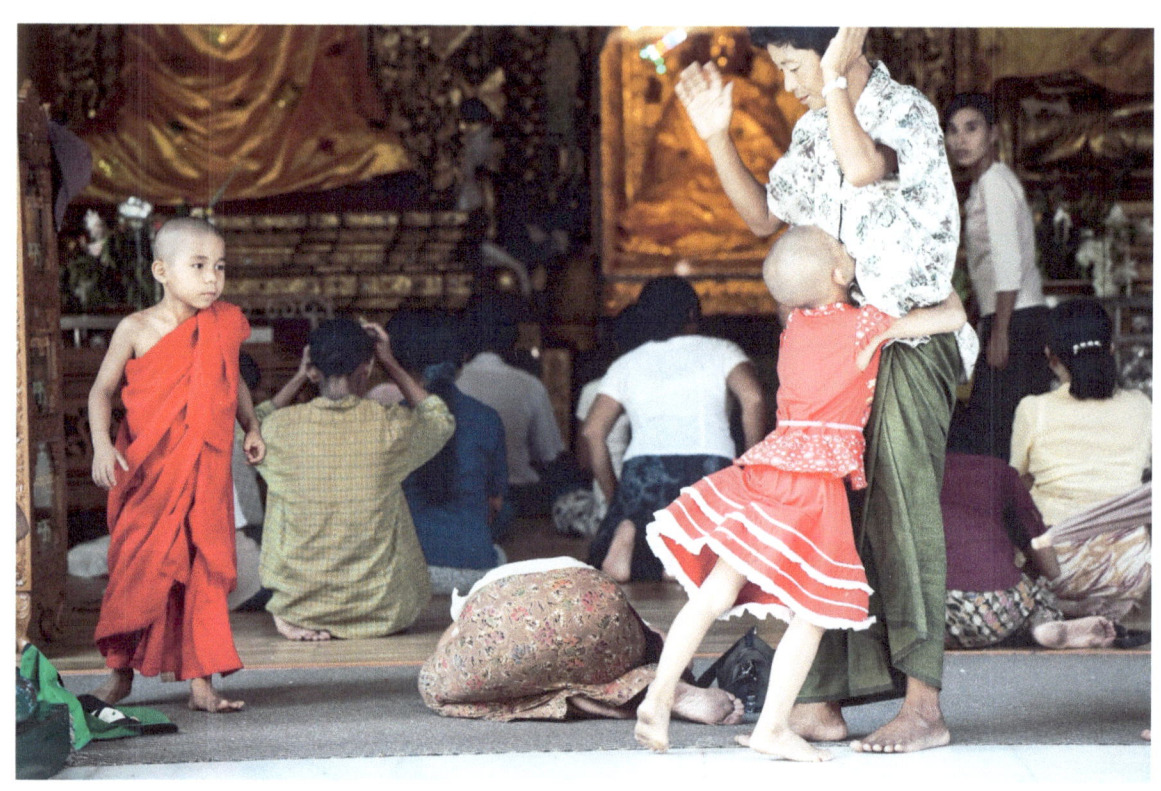

Child showing affection, Shwedagon Pagoda, Yangon, 2009

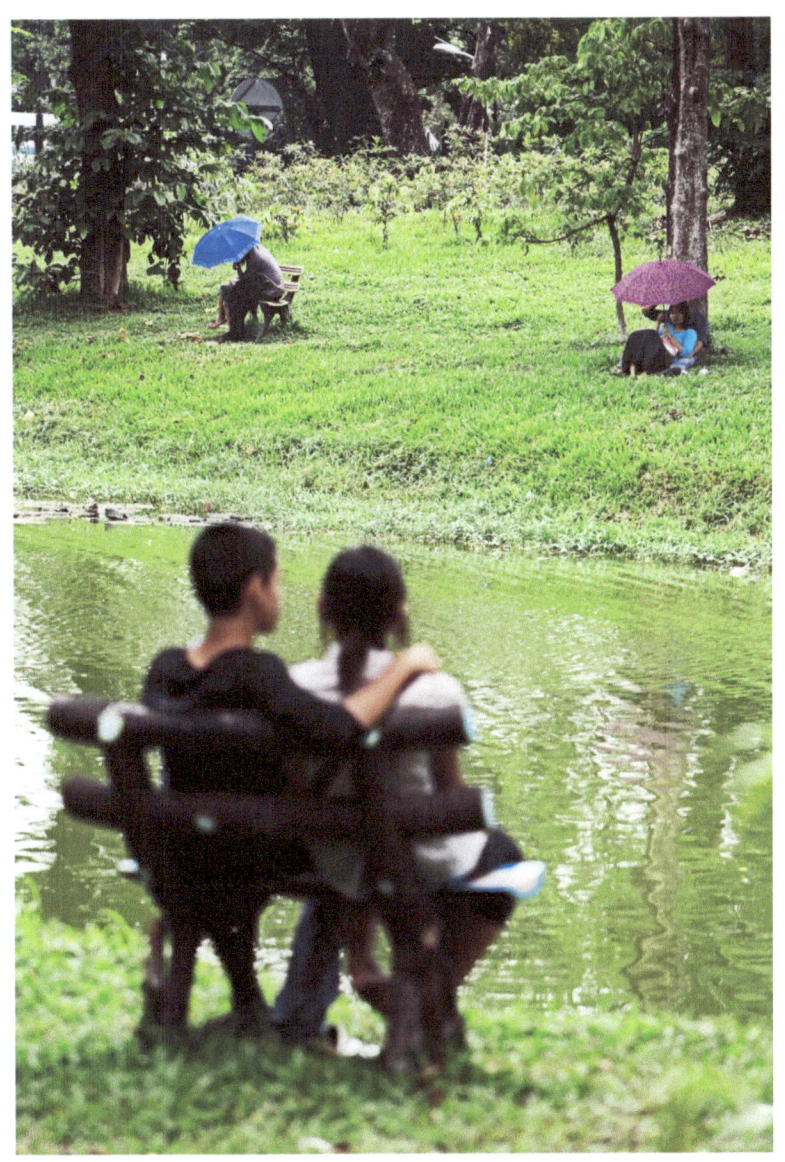

Courting Couples, Kandawgyi Lake, Yangon, 2009

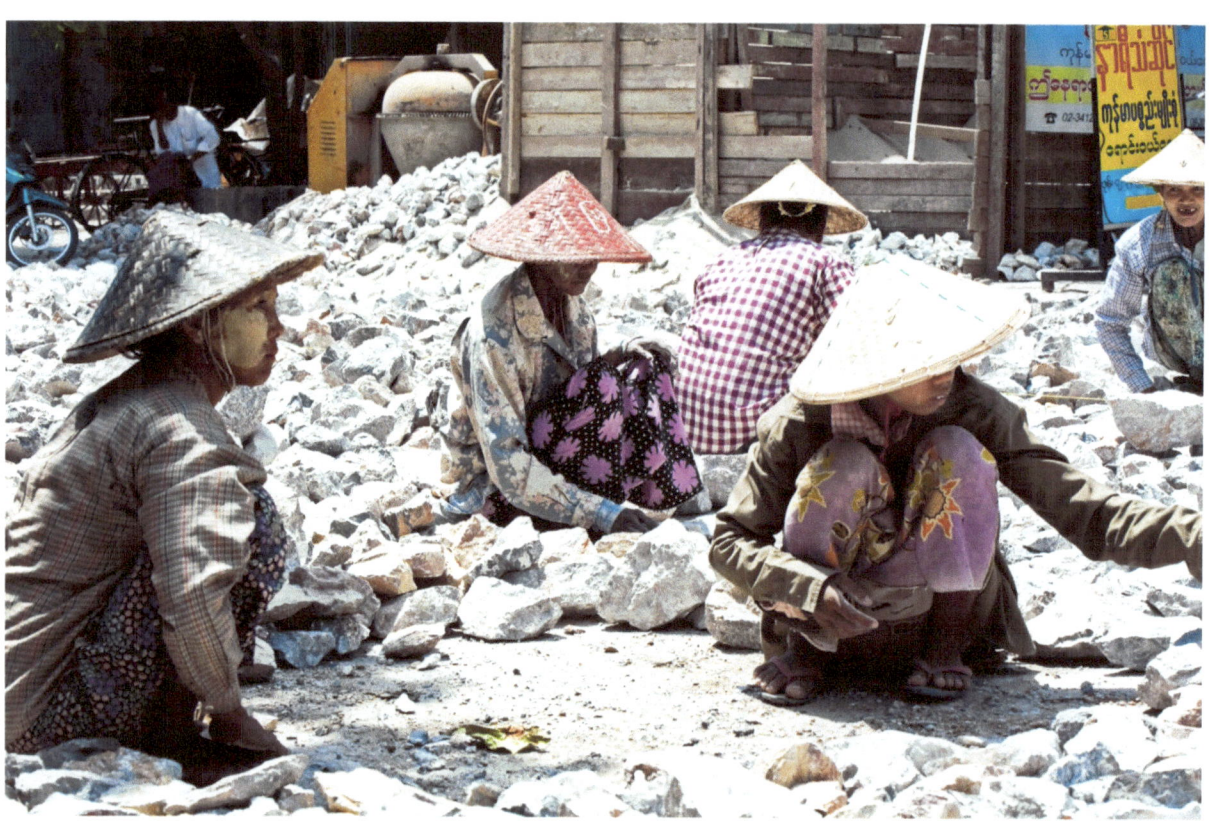

Labourers breaking rocks for road surface, Mandalay, 2009

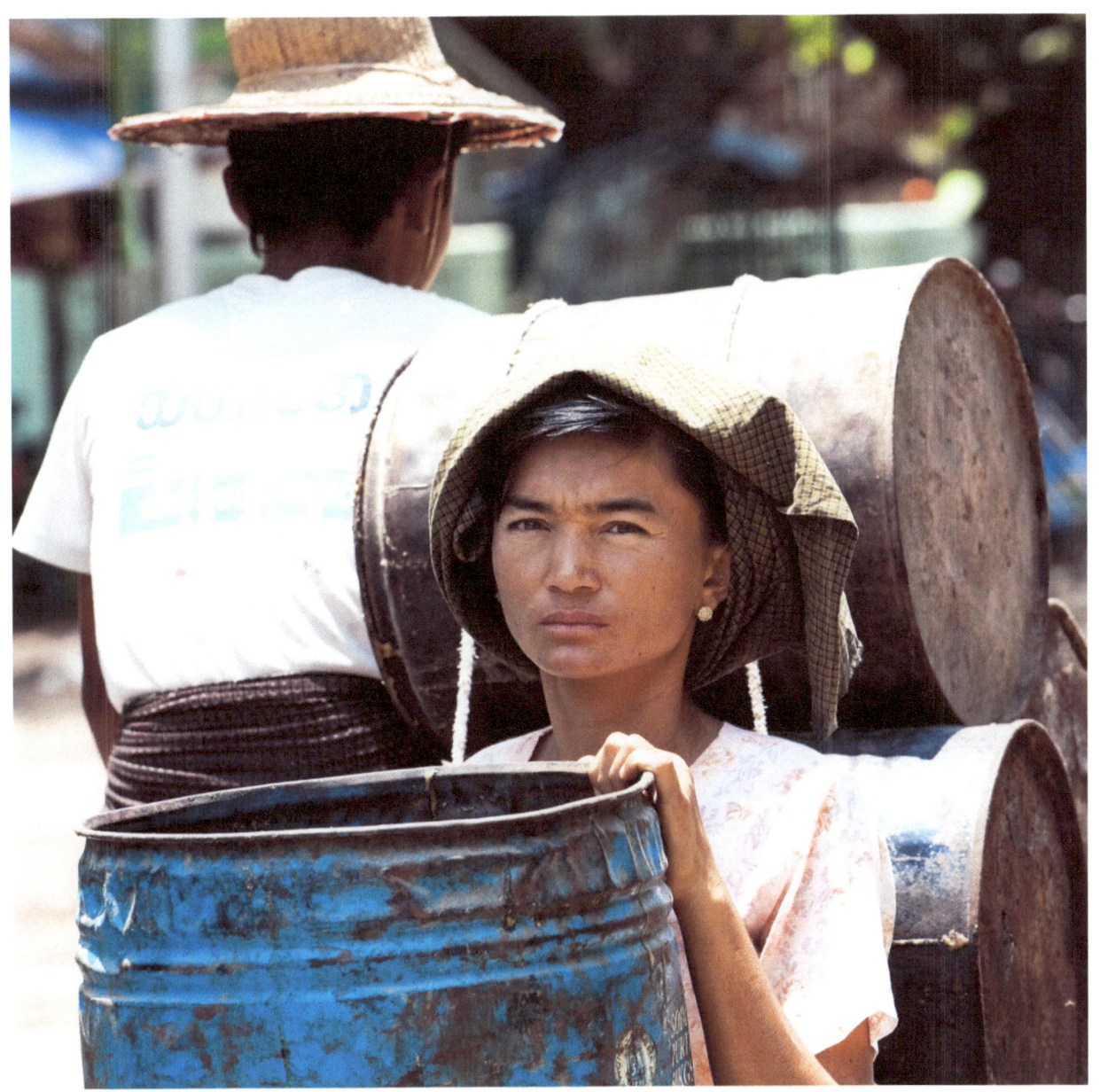
Female riding on back of rickshaw, Monywa, 2009

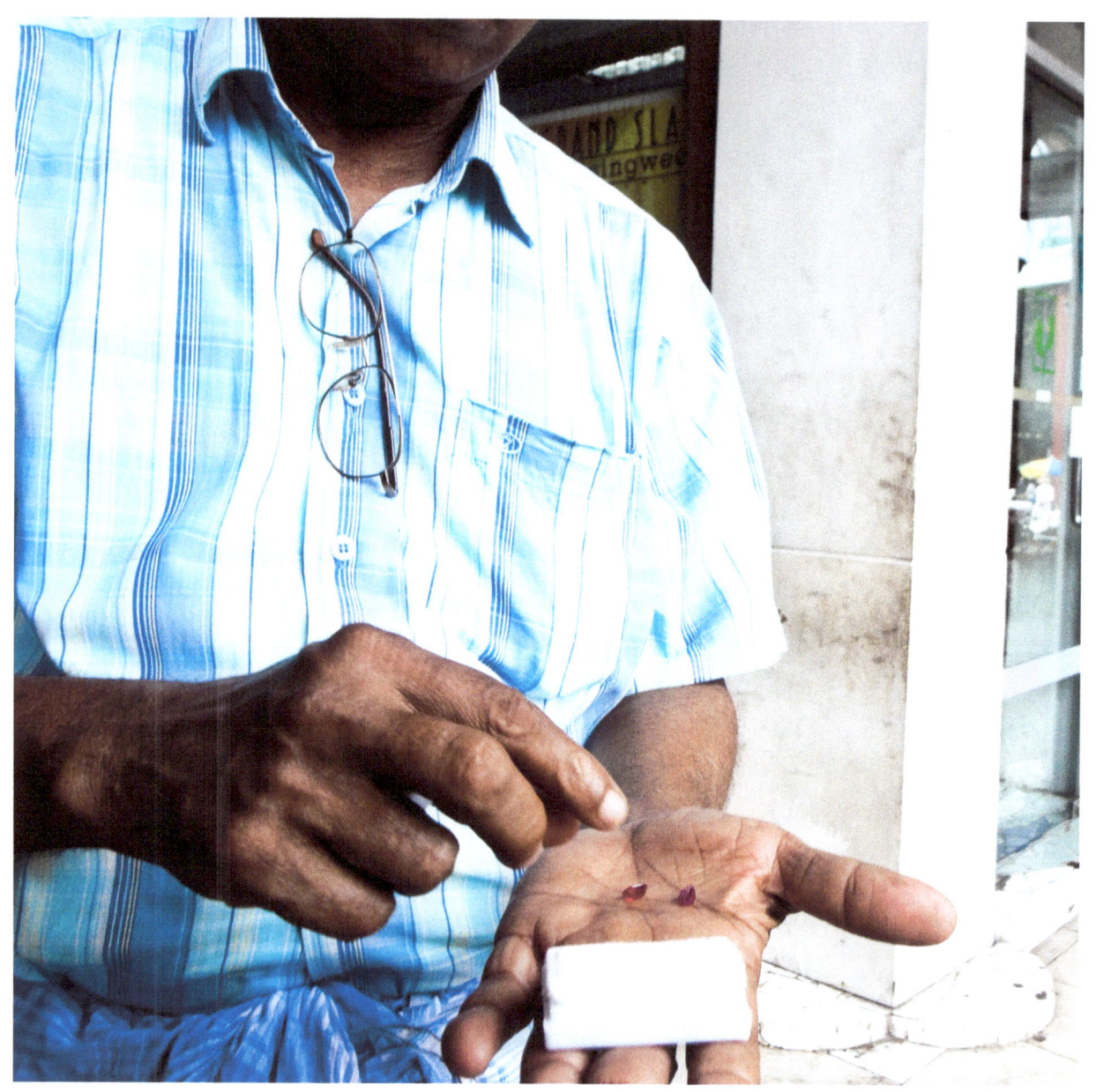

"Jewel" Seller, Yangon, 2009

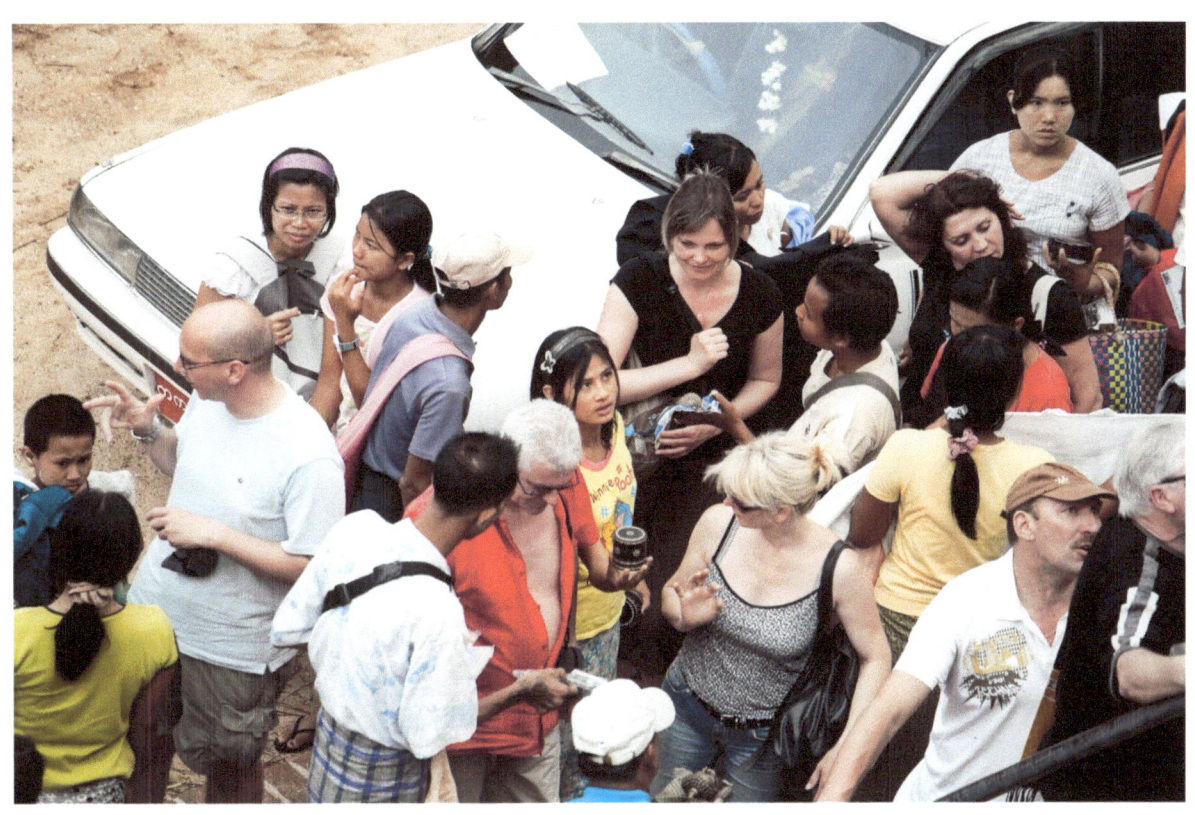

Hawkers crowding around tourists at Temple complex, Bagan, 2009

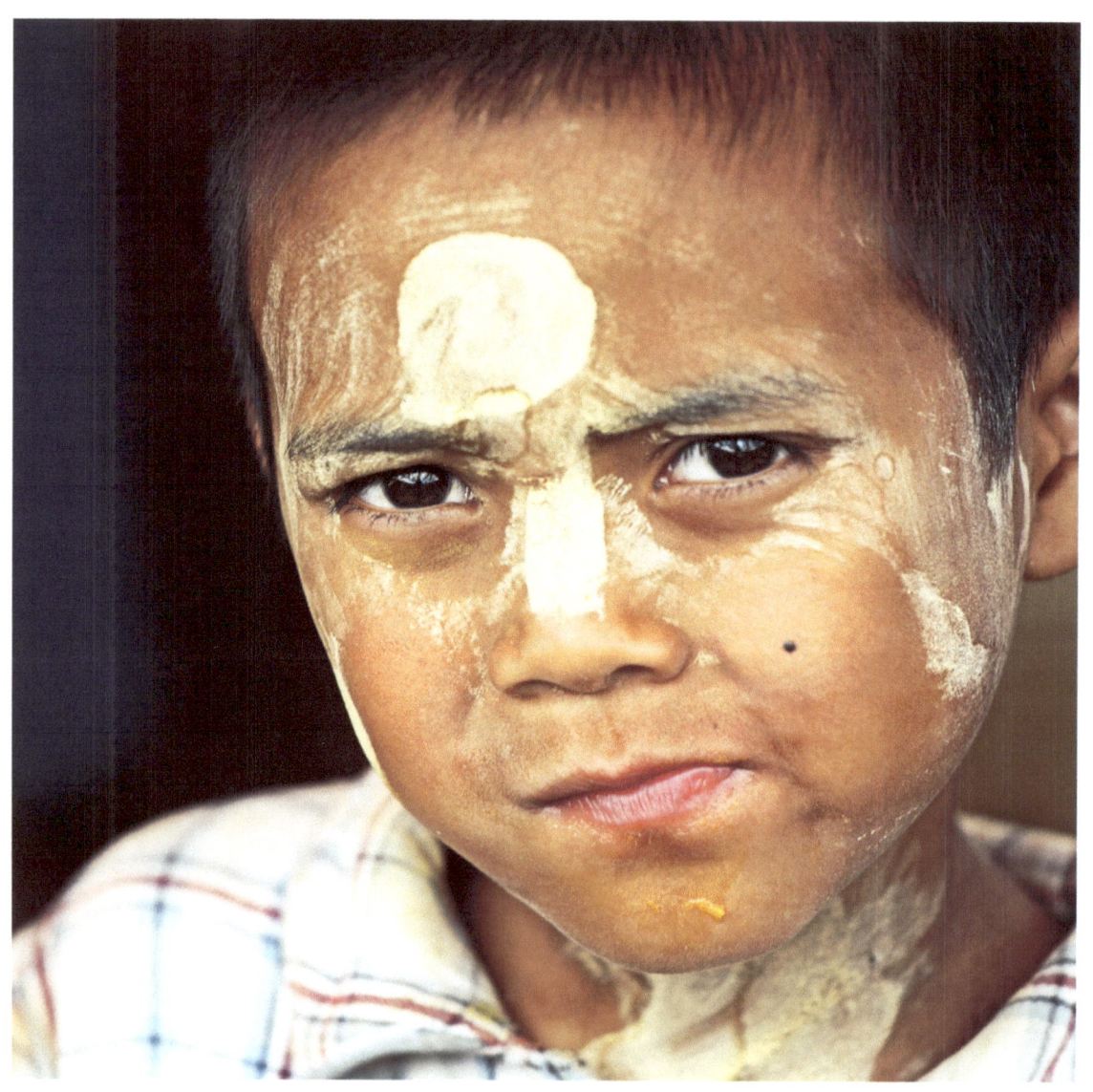

Boy at Market, Kalaw, Inle Lake, 2009

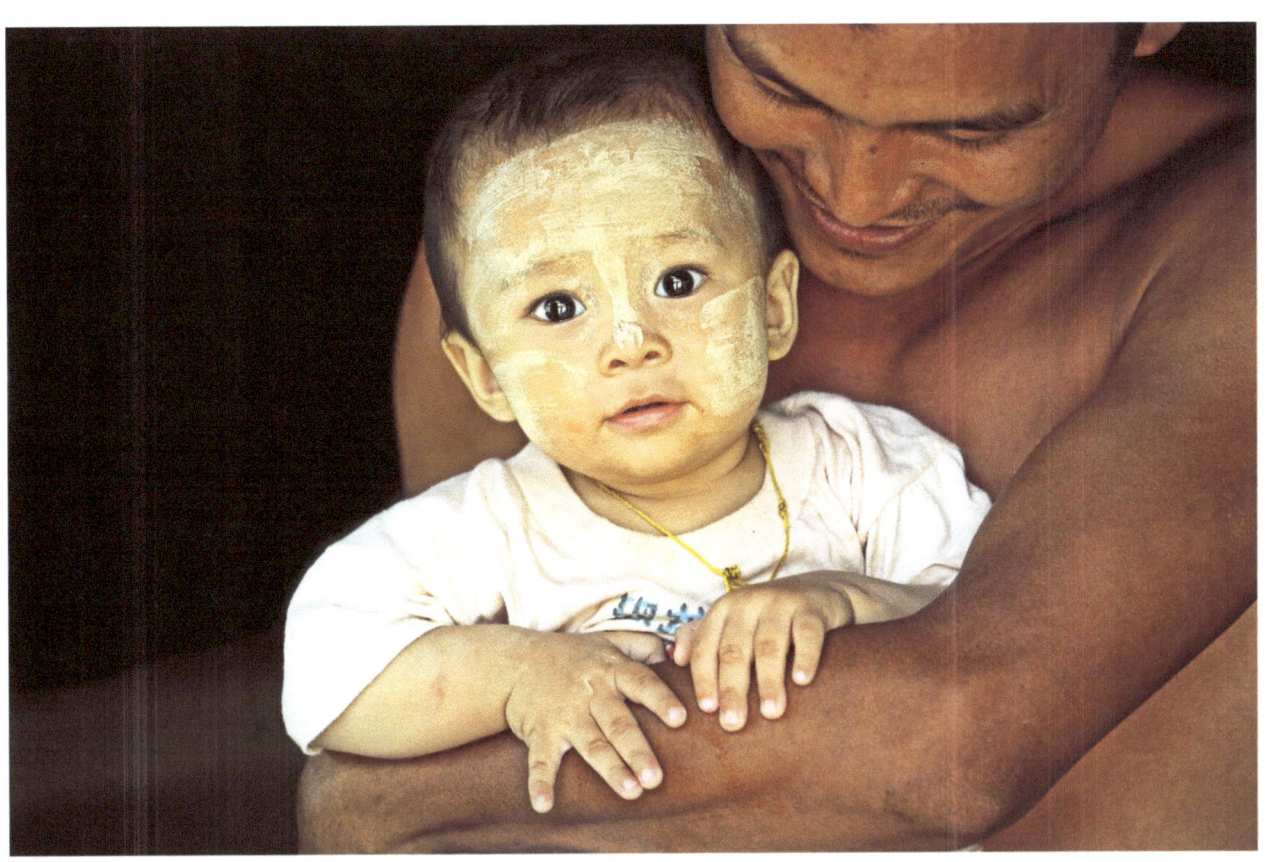

Father & Child outside home on the way to Inle Lake, 2009

www.ingramcontent.com/pod-product-compliance
Lightning Source LLC
Chambersburg PA
CBHW050733180526
45159CB00003B/1211

* 9 7 8 0 9 8 7 9 2 5 3 9 8 *